THE UNIVERSITY OF
WINCHESTER

Martial Rose Library
Tel: 01962 827306

To be returned on or before the day marked above, subject to recall.

Talking Back

Talking Back

Talking Back

The Idea of Civilization in the
India Nationalist Discourse

Sabyasachi Bhattacharya

OXFORD
UNIVERSITY PRESS

OXFORD
UNIVERSITY PRESS

Oxford University Press is a department of the University of Oxford.
It furthers the University's objective of excellence in research, scholarship,
and education by publishing worldwide. Oxford is a registered trademark of
Oxford University Press in the UK and in certain other countries

Published in India by
Oxford University Press
YMCA Library Building, 1 Jai Singh Road, New Delhi 110 001, India

ISBN-13: 978-0-19-807504-2
ISBN-10: 0-19-807504-9

Typeset in Sabon LT STD 10/12.6
by Sai Graphic Design, New Delhi 110 055
Printed in India at Rakmo Press, New Delhi 110 020

Contents

Abbreviations

BR	*Bankim Rachanavali*
CWMG	*Collected Works of Mahatma Gandhi*
CWSV	*Complete Works of Swami Vivekananda*
HS	*Hind Swaraj*
NAI	National Archives of India
PHISPC	Project of History of Indian Science, Philosophy and Culture
RR	*Rabindra Rachnavali*
SWJN	*Selected Works of Jawaharlal Nehru*

Introduction

The British discourse on India's history was by and large a monologue for the greater part of the nineteenth century. From around the turn of the century India began to talk back. About that time the colonial assumptions in imagining and narrating India's past began to be questioned by Indians. The contestation centred on the quality of pre-colonial Indian civilization vis-à-vis that of Europe, and the theme of India's unity and nationhood. Along with the discourse of nationhood, there developed a parallel discourse on civilization.

While the discourse of nationhood has received its share of attention, the civilizational discourse has not received historians' attention as much as it deserves. Indeed it was developed chiefly by men outside of the ranks of professional historians—by nationalist public spokesmen. Emerging from the embryonic form, in the writings of the generation of R.G. Bhandarkar (1837–1925) and Bankimchandra Chatterjee (1838–1894) in the late nineteenth century, the discourse of civilization appears fully fledged in Mahatma Gandhi's *Hind Swaraj* (published in 1909) and Rabindranath Tagore's early essays on the history of India (published from 1902 to 1907) and reaches its climactic form in Jawaharlal Nehru's *The Discovery of India* (published in 1946).

The two broad tendencies in this trend of thinking were, first, to talk back to the colonial masters in refutation of the disparagement of the ancient Indian civilization by colonial historians, and, second, to assert India's civilizational unity in the past. The first of these tendencies sometimes veered towards a vainglorious depiction of a 'Hindu civilization'; the second tended to posit a unity in civilizational terms almost as a surrogate for national unity, since nothing corresponding to the current European notion of nationhood could be established very far back in the past. 'Talking back' was evidently a reaction to the British colonial historians' adverse evaluation of Indian civilization. The second trend was a subtext in the discourse of nationhood, though only a few thinkers addressed specifically the issue of civilization. While Gandhi, Tagore, or Nehru were the foremost thought-leaders in the representation of Indian civilization in a new way, there were many others, mainly academic intellectuals in the areas of sociology, linguistics, intellectual history, and various branches of historiography, who contributed to make 'Indian civilization' a central theme in all forms of Indian studies.

In this book an attempt has been made to identify the main thrust of the consequent intellectual output. What was the point of this endeavour? What was said when Indians began to talk back? What was the discourse of civilization all about?

In the following pages I shall try to introduce the dramatis personae who appear on this stage. It will also serve to provide a chronological framework—necessary since the following chapters focus upon major themes and thinkers, and the thematic treatment cannot be consistently chronological. I dispense with references in these introductory pages since the references and citations are mentioned in the chapters which follow.

* * *

It is well known that James Mill's history of India and his adverse evaluation of Indian civilization marked a watershed. It was a departure from the early Orientalists' approach. Sir William Jones (1746–1794), one of the earliest Orientalists, was a great admirer of ancient Indian civilization and his translations of some classics of those times were avidly read by leading contemporary intellectuals, including Goethe and Schiller. James Mill (1773–1836) was critical of that approach for he believed that in the 'scale of civilization' Indians stood at a low level if one considered their laws and institutions and the arts and sciences in the past. As a Utilitarian ideologue and an important official in the East India Company, Mill was extremely influential. His history moulded the minds of generations of British members of the Indian Civil Service since Mill's history was a textbook in their training school at Haileybury. Mill knew no Indian language nor did he ever visit India, and in the later editions of his book, the editor, H.H. Wilson, pointed out numerous errors in Mill's historical narrative. Nevertheless, Mill's book retained its reputation as a 'classic' and had a formative influence on colonial historiography after his times. He influenced British imagination of India and her past. Chapter 1 in this book addresses the question: how did the early generation of Indian intellectuals exposed to 'English Knowledge' in the new universities created in 1857–8, respond to the disparagement of Indian civilization? We have studied in detail the writings of two representative individuals, Bankimchandra Chatterjee and R.G. Bhandarkar who were born about the same time and were among the first batch of students to graduate from the universities of Calcutta and Bombay. Prior to that, some of those exposed to 'English education' at the undergraduate level in Hindu College in Calcutta show a critical awareness of the writings of Mill and colonial historians who followed. But it was the generation of Chatterjee and Bhandarkar who acquired requisite familiarity with methods of modern critical scholarship, distinct from the methods and approach of the traditional intellectuals, the pandits and the maulavis. That is why the first chapter is titled 'The Colonialist Monologue and India Talking Back'.

The first tract Gandhi published, *Hind Swaraj* (1909) marks the opening of a truly nationalist discourse of civilization. India, he said, need not have the expulsion of the British as the aim, India could accommodate them, but not Western civilization. Thus it was an unusual political tract which subordinated the political agenda to the civilizational discourse. In Chapter 2 an attempt has been made to analyse Gandhi's highly complex ideas in this regard, with *Hind Swaraj* as the text in focus. The centrality of this text in the total corpus of Gandhi's writings is generally recognized. In many respects it anticipates Gandhi's future agenda of action and line of thinking. For instance, Gandhi speaks of an 'Indian civilization' and not a 'Hindu civilization'. Gandhi anticipates the nationalist ideology of a pluralist reconciliation of diversities in saying, India has 'the faculty of assimilation'. Above all, Gandhi's denunciation of Western civilization in *Hind Swaraj* addressed the sentiment widely prevalent in India in respect of the perceived disparagement of Indian civilization in the colonialist discourse.

A few years before *Hind Swaraj* was published, Rabindranath Tagore offered a view of Indian civilization which later formed the basis of a full-fledged nationalist paradigm: the 'syncretic' civilization of India. In an essay, 'The History of Bharatvarsha', published in 1902, Tagore argued that India's aim through the ages has been 'to establish unity amidst diversity', without eliminating the uniqueness of each element. In 1912, Tagore elaborated this notion further and postulated that while India's endeavour has been to bring about unity through cultural assimilation, Western civilization has been characterized by self-aggrandizement and suppression of diversity by means of state power. He cited the example of imperialist expansion as well as the fate of aboriginals in North America, Australia, New Zealand, and South Africa. As we shall see in Chapter 3, while Tagore's idea of India's 'syncretic civilization' was incorporated in the nationalist ideology, Tagore moved increasingly towards a highly critical stance in respect of nationalism inspired by Western ideas and history. He believed that the 'organized selfishness' of nationalism was alien to Indian civilization. To a good number of people in the nationalist camp this was rank apostasy. Another difference between Tagore's approach and the nationalist position was in respect of the encounter of Indian civilization with Western civilization, Tagore's willingness to acknowledge India's debt to the intellectually regenerative role of the Western impact, as well as his diatribes against nationalism made him a problematic presence in the margins of the nationalist movement in the 1920s and 1930s.

Soon after Tagore developed the notion of syncretic unity amidst diversities in Indian civilization (1902) and Gandhi the idea of the superiority of Indian civilization (1909), a number of other observers put forward analogous ideas. Radha Kumud Mookerji (1884–1963) expounded the idea of 'the Fundamental Unity of India' (1914) on the basis of citations from Hindu scriptures, legends concerning pilgrimage sites all over India, the attribution of 'universal' sovereignty in adulatory memorials to kings, and so on. Vincent Smith in an introduction to the *Oxford History of India* (1919) postulated India's 'unity in diversity'. However, these were approaches to the notion of unity in a perspective different from that of Tagore's and Gandhi's. Vincent Smith and Mookerji saw unity in 'Hindu India' and they also underlined this geographical unity in the subcontinent. They did not postulate a process of syncretism or assimilation; in fact, Smith specifically rejected that possibility and Mookerji did not touch upon that question at all.

The idea that Hinduism provided the unifying element—indeed that it was the basis of nationhood—had other proponents in the early twentieth century. In Vinayak Damodar Savarkar's (1883–1966) writings the concept of the Hindu civilization recurs quite often. While in Vincent Smith's political imagination the unity imparted by Hinduism to diverse peoples in India did not imply nationhood, to Savarkar that unity was the basis of nationhood—to the exclusion of all outside the pale of Hinduism (Chapter 5).

In fact the search for a sacred India, an unchanging foundational basis of the civilization, was not limited to the communally minded. It is possible to argue on the following lines: History is a colonial evil which originated in India's discovery of the temporality of the world. The exit from the sacred timelessness created a vacuum. A sacred eternal India was needed to fill up that vacuum. This psychological need was met by the discourse of civilization. It was immaterial whether such an India existed in the past, it was a necessity in the present times. However, this view of the late nineteenth and early twentieth century India does not form a part of our argument here. That line of argument may help explain the acceptance of a Hindu view of Indian civilization, but it has little to do with the nationalist paradigm of an assimilative civilization bridging diversity of faiths and cultures. In the early years of the twentieth century some intellectuals, with or without explicit nationalist affiliation, created a wave of historical consciousness in some parts of India. This found expression in regional histories as well as in that genre of literature which is known as historical fiction, the border between the two being at times a little fuzzy. This happened in several linguistic regions. In Chapter 4 we look at two most prominent instances, Maharashtra and Bengal. In Bombay and Pune there developed an 'archival movement', an effort to preserve and access historical records and thus to reconstruct Maratha history. Two outstanding leaders in this field were Mahadev Govinda Ranade (1842–1901) and V.K. Rajwade (1863–1926). Ranade not only played an important role in pressuring the Bombay Government to open the archives of the *Peshwa Daftar*, but also wrote a well-documented history of the *Rise of the Maratha Power* (1901). He saw in that history the 'first beginning of the process of nation-making'. Ranade and Rajwade, and the two organizations they started, Bharatiya Itihas Samsodhak Mandal and Deccan Vernacular Translation Society, created a kind of historical consciousness which drew support from and contributed to regional as well as Indian identity consciousness. In Bengal, we can look at Akshay Kumar Maitreya (1861–1930) as a similar representative figure. Maitreya, among others, made heroic attempts to contest colonial historians' account of the East India Company's conquest of Bengal. About the time when Ranade was trying to review Shivaji's place in history, Maitreya focused his research work on *Sirajuddoula* (1898), the last independent Nawab of Bengal. He also launched journals of popular history in the

Bengali language and founded the first historical research society in Bengal—an organization of 'native' intellectuals, as distinct from the Asiatic Society in Calcutta which was controlled by Englishmen in the Indian Civil Service. Rabindranath Tagore wrote in 1898–9 three essays on Maitreya's historical work and he saw in it a sign that Indians had developed a 'hunger for history' and a historical consciousness. Nationalist historiography worked towards merging the regional with a national identity consciousness in the discourse of history.

About the time when Ranade began to write his essays on the rise of Maratha power and Maitreya his essays on Bengal's history, Vivekananda appeared in the forum of the global Parliament of Religions in Chicago (1893). Swami Vivekananda (1863–1902), earlier known as Narendranath Dutta, in his brief meteoric career in the next ten years, staunchly contested some of the stereotypical representations of the 'spiritual' Indian civilization; he emphasized the need for an equilibrium between the supposedly spiritual and the materialistic domains. Jawaharlal Nehru cited his writings profusely in *The Discovery of India,* possibly in recognition of the formative influence of Vivekananda on the Indian mind in Nehru's times. Having worked with a great missionary zeal in North America and England for several years, to propagate his neo-Vedantic philosophy, Vivekananda was convinced of the need to negotiate with Western civilization, to learn from it; at the same time he warned his people against being overwhelmed by it. He also preached what we describe as Theistic Universalism, distinct from the secular universalism of the Nehruvian kind. That notion was derived from his faith in the essential unity of all religions. Aurobindo (1872–1950), earlier known as Aurobindo Ghose, an ideological leader of the militant nationalists, expounded an approach to Indian civilization at a high intellectual plain. From around 1918 onwards in a series of writings he challenged the Western critique of India's civilization. That was not uncommon, but what was remarkable was that, at least in his early writings from his retreat in Pondicherry, he distanced himself from the commonly accepted 'spiritual' interpretation of Indian culture. Spirituality might be the 'master key' to the Indian mind, but its exaggeration in the Occidental mind, he said, was due to a failure to appreciate the intellectuality and the vital force evinced in Indian civilization in the arts, architecture, legal and political thought, grammar, mathematical sciences, music, and indeed in all the 'sixty-four accomplishments' ranging from dancing to horse-breeding. Although Aurobindo's abstract analytical style of thinking is different from that of Vivekananda's, they both underline what they perceive as the state of decline of a great civilization in India and the consequent need for a reconstruction, which can be achieved only by absorbing Western modernity without being possessed or overcome by it. It is not surprising that in *The Discovery of India* Vivekananda is described as a bridge between the past of India and the present.

In the exposition of the paradigm of civilization we have examined a running theme has been an unresolved antinomy right from the beginning between an openness to Western civilization and the wholesale rejection of it. It was left to Jawaharlal Nehru, on the eve of Independence, once again to try and reconcile these two approaches. This is what we look at in Chapter 4. In a sense, he represented himself to be an exemplar of that reconciliation. He begins the *The Discovery of India* with a confession: he was a child, he said, of Asia with her tradition in his blood, and at the same time he looked upon himself as a foster-child of the Western world. That divided self was not untypical of the Indian intelligentsia of the early twentieth century and that is his vantage point when he begins to explore the question he poses in the first few pages of that book: What is this India? Nehru is critical of the India that was left behind the times and fell prey to the British. At the same time he looks to the India that there was, on a par if not ahead of Europe till the eighteenth century. Nehru acknowledges what India gained from the challenge of the West, and at the same time he recognizes the other, the exploitative face of the West in Asia. On the whole his position is close to Tagore's. The central thesis of the book, if there is any, is the argument taken over from Gandhi and Tagore, the significance of the unity of India's civilization amidst diversity. The consequent pluralist approach was made by Jawaharlal Nehru and his peers— most notably Abul Kalam Azad (1858–1968) a foundational idea in shaping the policies of the post-Independence state. In the 1960s nationalist intellectual stalwarts like M. Mujeeb (*Indian Muslims*, 1962) or S. Abid Hussain (*The Destiny of Indian Muslims*, 1965) developed this line of thinking into a well-articulated ideological position.

It is easy to pick holes in the nationalist representation of Indian civilization. We look at some of its problems and infirmities in Chapter 5. The assumption of continuity in that civilization does not stand scrutiny if we are looking for continuity in terms of location in a territorially defined political unit over a long period. Second, there is also a problem with 'unity' conceived in terms of certain foundational characteristics or as immanent unchanging personality of the civilization. It is difficult to identify an agency which is the carrier of these supposed foundational characteristics which impart unity. Sardar K.M. Panikkar (1896–1963) speculated that the unifying 'steel framework' of the civilization was in the social regulation prescribed in the Dharmashastras, and their interpretation and adjustment. That conservative amendment to the classical nationalist interpretation was not widely accepted or even noticed. That leads us to the third debated issue: Variants of the nationalist paradigm of civilization have been often employed to serve a 'Hindu' interpretation of India's Hindu past. V.D. Savarkar (1883–1966) was a spokesman of that point of view, particularly in this advocacy of the notion of a 'Hindu nation'. Finally, there is also a kind of incompleteness by design in the classical nationalist view. D.D. Kosambi (1907–1966) accepted the nationalist notions of continuity in Indian civilizations for 3,000 years, as well as the dialectics of forces working towards unity and diversity. But he found the nationalist exposition, for example, Nehru's *The Discovery of India*, wanting in class analysis, and in its inattention to the material basis of civilization. In Chapter 5 an attempt is made to review the critique of the nationalist discourse of civilization from these different points of view.

It is very curious that the academic historians in India scarcely responded to the civilizational discourse in twentieth century Europe. It is true that Oswald Spengler (1880–1936) had little to say about the eastern civilizations in *The Decline of the West* (1918), but he posited a 'comparative morphology of world history' and a 100 years after James Mill he projected the inevitable decline of the Western civilization which Mill had held up as the ultimate end of history. Likewise Arnold Toynbee (1889–1975) from 1934 onwards wrote in his ten stout volumes of the history of civilizations, an unstated message: it was the recognition of a plurality of civilizational trajectories of development, replacing the nineteenth century linear conception of all civilizations progressing towards the European pattern. But academic historians in India remained unresponsive; 'civilization' as a category was not in the professional historians' bag of tools in Indian universities. After this signal failure in the early half of the twentieth century, in the second half of the century Indian mind in the academia entered the discourse of civilization by diverse routes. In anthropology and sociology G.S. Ghurye (1893–1983) and Nirmal Kumar Bose (1901–72) opened up the study of Indian civilization on synchronic lines, in conjunction with the historians' diachronic study. In part this was part of the intellectual impact of the work of A.L. Kroeber (1876–1958) and Robert Redfield (1897–1958). In part it was an autonomous development of the Indian mind introspecting on India's culture in making. A space was created for a new ethno-historical approach to India's civilization.

Another route to civilizational concerns was the burgeoning literature on nationalism inspired by the works of Ernest Gellner (*Nations and Nationalism*, 1983), Benedict Anderson (*Imagined Communities: Reflections on the Origin and Spread of Nationalism*, 1983), or Eric Hobsbawm (*Nations and Nationalisms Since 1780: Programme, Myth, Reality*, 1992). The installation of nationalism in a central place in political studies brought in its wake a greater awareness of the historicity of nations as civilizations, that is, the continuity and unity of a cultural kind in the long run of history. Although somewhat far removed from this genre of writing, in telescoping the national with the civilizational, the *reductio ad absurdum* was reached in Samuel P. Huntington's speculations on 'civilization paradigm' in his work on *Clash of Civilizations* (1996).

A third route to the theme of civilizations was travelled in recent decades by historians of culture. The enormous literature spawned by the debate on Edward Said's seminal work *Orientalism* (1978) can be read as the long-awaited answer from Eastern civilizations which suffered from the Eurocentric discourse of power which had been represented as evaluation of those civilizations in colonial hands. Said says that being 'Oriental as a child' in the British colonies of Egypt and Palestine, he had the experience of being subjected to the same 'nexus of knowledge and power' which the subject people experienced in India and other colonies. While Said's Foucauldian argument went way beyond the nationalist intellectuals' critique of early twentieth century vintage, the subtext of that critique resonated with the cast of mind created by the nationalist critique. This was probably a factor in the reception of Said's thesis in Asian countries. Said put back 'civilization' as a category of thought in historiography. We have reviewed in Chapter 5 the consequent impact.

There are several other issues which we touch upon in the last chapter. A major revision in historiography in recent years has been to contest the view of James Mill and colonial historians that in ancient India there was no sense of the historical. Romila Thapar looks to the recovery of history embedded in the *itihasa–purana* tradition. Likewise Anthony K. Warder, David Shulman, Sanjay Subrahmanyam, among others, see in pre-modern writings not only sources from which history is to be recovered, but also a genre of writings which are in themselves works of history. Another issue is addressed by Dipesh Chakrabarty in *Provincializing Europe* (2001) when he makes the point that the master narrative of European history, centralizing the nation state, so dominates historical imagination globally, Indian history is 'bound to represent a sad figure of lack and failure'. However, he does not consider the Indian endeavour to construct an alternative narrative in civilizational terms; we have argued in this book that this endeavour merits attention. Prior to Chakrabarty, Ashis Nandy in a path-breaking essay of 1995 also underlined the link between the very idea of history and the modern nation state and the export of the Western historical worldview of history to the rest of the world. But Nandy arrives at a conclusion somewhat different from Chakrabarty's: Nandy persuasively argues for ahistoricity as an escape route from the trap of the Western worldview of history. Amartya Sen's intervention in the discourse in an essay, *On Interpreting India's Past* (1996), has unfortunately received little attention. How objective was the nationalist interpretation of India's civilization and history? Sen takes an epistemological position which enables a defence of that interpretation. He argues that observations which are sometimes readily condemned as subjective are not necessarily so, because these may be observations which are objective in terms of the position of observation. Apart from this notion of 'positional objectivity', Sen also argues for an evaluation of these observations in terms of 'practical reason', that is, the social and political implications of those observations in terms of action. Sen's ideas in this regard have been elaborated later in his work on *The Idea of Justice* (2009). On the whole, there has been a good deal of fecund thinking on civilization in India in the recent years and that is the theme of the last chapter in this book, 'Rethinking Indian Civilization'.

It has not been our aim in this book to make an exhaustive inventory of all that has been said about India's civilization. That would have been a pointless exercise for the chief question proposed here is: why did India need to develop a discourse of civilization? We are so familiar with the representation of India as a great civilization which brings about a unity amidst diversities, and accommodates in the Indian polity a pluralistic society, that we take the Indian discourse of civilization for granted. How mistaken we are in taking that for granted will be obvious if we look at some other Third World countries where such an accommodating concept of civilization is not the generally accepted currency of the realm. And it is equally instructive to look at the European discourse of nationhood, where the concept of civilization does not figure so prominently. In late nineteenth and early twentieth century India, the concept of civilization developed because in the process of nation building, appeal to a civilizational unity was a necessity, given the fact that the unifying factors present in the west European nation states since the fifteenth century were missing in the Indian subcontinent. The discourse of civilization was needed in India to make nationhood thinkable.

CHAPTER 1

The Colonialist
Monologue and India
Talking Back

The representation of India's civilization in the colonial writings has a long history. No doubt the issue was problematized in a variety of ways from colonial times onwards, but the outcome as a totality has been a rich scholarly tradition of studying 'Orientalist' writings.[1] The impact of the paradigmatic change brought about by Edward Said has affected the interpretative stance of many recent scholars in that tradition but the empirical foundations built over several decades survive as a narrative resource.[2]

The moment in that narrative which merits our attention in the present context is the termination of the era dominated by Sir William Jones and the installation of a new narrative pattern through the writings of James Mill from roughly the second

decade of the nineteenth century. The first three volumes of Mill's
History of India were published in 1817.³ James Mill reacted very
strongly against the admiring attitude of Sir William Jones and his
contemporary Orientalists towards the ancient Indian civilization.
For instance, Mill cites Jones's statement on the works of Kalidasa
which Jones translated into English (and these translations were also
admiringly read by men like Goethe and Schiller in Europe). Jones
had written that even in the first century BC, Hindu Kings 'gave
encouragement to poets, philologers [*sic*] and mathematicians, at
a time when the Britons were as unlettered and unpolished as the
army of Hanumat.'⁴ Mill contested this view sedulously: 'It was
unfortunate that Sir William Jones should have adopted the hypothesis of a high stage of civilization in the principal countries of Asia.'
According to Mill, the motivation actuating Jones was 'the virtuous
design of exalting the Hindus in the eyes of their European masters, and hence ameliorating the temper of the government.'⁵ To this
explanation of the admiration exhibited by Jones and some others,
James Mill added another possible explanation. Hindu civilization
had been exalted by the early Orientalists because of the contrast
between India and the North American indigenous population.
'The nations of Europe became acquainted, nearly about the same
period, with the people of America and the people of Hindustan....
The Hindus were compared with the savages of America' and thus a
conclusion 'too favourable' to the Hindus was arrived at—although
in reality, Mill observed, the Hindus were in a state 'little removed
from that of half-civilised nations.'⁶ Mill goes on to say that it was
obvious to observers in the eighteenth century that Indians were not
as civilized at that time as they were at one time supposed to be in
the Orientalists' imagination. And therefore it was often argued by
Orientalist adulators of India that Hindus had declined in the scale
of civilization, that they had descended to a 'stage of degradation'
due to 'foreign conquest and subjugation'. Mill rejected this argument. According to him, 'We know of no such period of calamity
as was sufficient to reduce them to a state of ignorance and barbar-
ity'; Muslim conquest was 'to no extraordinary degree sanguinary

or destructive.'[7] Thus Mill totally dismissed the positive evaluation of ancient Indian civilization by Sir William Jones and some of his contemporaries in the eighteenth century.

Mill was of the view that India had never attained the high state of civilization the Orientalists had imagined and in the early nineteenth century there was abundant evidence of 'the ignorance of the Hindus and the low stage of civilisation in which they remain.'[8] It is interesting to see that as a major evidence of the low state of civilization of the Hindus, Mill cited the lack of historical works. Poetry, admired by Jones and the like, could be produced by people relatively uncivilized. But 'a degree of culture is needed', Mill said, to produce works of history and in this the Hindus failed. 'It is allowed on all hands that no historical composition existed in the literature of the Hindus; they had not reached that point of intellectual maturity at which the value of a record of the past for the guidance of the future begins to be understood.'[9] To James Mill it was clear as a syllogism: A civilized people wrote history, the Hindus wrote no history, therefore they were not civilized.

James Mill knew no Indian language, he had never been to India, and his history contained many factual errors which were pointed out by H.H. Wilson when he edited Mill's history in 1844. However, he framed his agenda of writing *History of British India* very ambitiously and the early part of the multivolume history included pre-colonial India. Although purportedly limited to the history of British India, Mill's history devoted the whole of Book I to an evaluation of 'Hindu civilization' on the basis of a few translations of ancient texts and accounts written by European travellers and East India Company officials, mainly of the eighteenth century. His comments in chapter VI on religious texts were too amateurish to merit any comment, but chapter VII on 'Manners', that is, social and behavioural characteristics attributed to Indians, usually aggregated as 'the Hindus', were interesting. To reproduce the subtitles in that chapter will suffice: 'Proneness to Adulation, Perjury, Inhospitality, Cruelty and Ferocity, Timidity, Litigiousness, Proneness to Foul Language, Love of Repose, Avarice....' In the next chapter Mill discusses 'the Arts' and his assessment was that Europeans who marvelled at the old Indian architectural and sculptural creations forget that 'arts of the barbarians' can also be impressive, that was not a sign of a high civilization. He cited the examples of the remains of the Aztecs in Mexico, the Incas of Peru, and the monarchs of ancient Egypt. With the exception of the artisanal production of cotton textiles Mill did not find any art worthy of being considered of high quality. Mill turned to literature in chapter IX and argued that the early Orientalists like Sir William Jones overrated ancient Indian literature. While he rejected that opinion, Mill must have been aware that it would have been unwise to pit himself against authorities like Jones—indeed Mill depended wholly on the translations made by the scholars he criticized. Mill had to be content with making sarcastic innuendos. He cites Adam Smith as an authority since he had also doubted whether there was any proof of high attainments among the 'ancient nations'. At the end of Book II (chapter V) of volume I, Mill returned to the theme of the backwardness of 'Hindu' civilization in a chapter entitled 'Comparison of the State of Civilization among the Muhammedan Conquerors of India with the State of Civilization among the Hindus'. That took care of the hypothesis of those who were prone to claim that although the Hindus were not at a high level in 'the scale of civilization' in the late eighteenth or early nineteenth century, that was a result of decline they experienced after the so-called 'Muslim conquest.' Jones rejected that hypothesis.

Having dismissed the false notion of some European observers, notably Sir William Jones and Orientalist scholars of his generation, regarding the high level of Hindu civilization, Mill expounded his own views on the subject. He believed in a hierarchy of civilizations distinguishing the higher from the lower ones. The point was to look at the 'stages of social progress', and the 'relative position of nations ... in the scale of civilisation.'[10] This notion of scale of civilization was important in British intellectual history; in later times this notion became a part of Social Darwinism and the evolutionary notion of civilizations of the world slowly progressing towards the peak represented by imperial Great Britain. Mill anticipates many later historians in pointing out that India had not attained unity for any considerable length of time and he quotes Rennell, a curious choice of an authority, who wrote: 'Rebellions, massacres and barbarous conquests make up the history of this fair country.'[11] Thus the opportunity to get truly civilized, a state of unity and peace, being conspicuously lacking, India could not go ahead in the 'scale of civilisation', judging by the criteria Mill applied, viz. 'laws and institutions which they framed, the manners they adopted, and the arts and science which they attended.'[12]

Why did these questions matter to Mill? It was because, first he differed from Sir William Jones's assessment of the 'pretended state of civilisation' claimed by Indians. Second, it was 'an object of highest practical importance' to the British who ruled India 'to ascertain the true state of the Hindu in the scale of civilisation.'[13] India was after all, Mill stated in the first page of his first volume, the 'great scene of British action.' And Mill was writing no ordinary history but 'a critical history...a judging history.'[14]

While his Indian readers reacted very adversely to Mill's evaluation of Indian civilization, we need to appreciate that it is necessary to situate Mill in his times to understand his approach. What did the world look like when James Mill passed his judgement about Indian civilization? By the first decade of the nineteenth century British rule in India had stabilized considerably and was about to enter a new period of expansion. By 1815, in Europe, Britain was not only established as a global power, after Britain's victory over Napoleon and France, but Britain had also undergone the first Industrial Revolution and had emerged as the most industrialized country in the world. Britain's confidence in being at the top of the world was nowhere better displayed than in British writings on India, a country she dominated and regarded as backward. Just about this time, in 1817 James Mill published a series of volumes on the history of India and this work had a formative influence on British imagination about India. The book was entitled *History of British India,* but the early part of the book included a survey of ancient and medieval

India while the later ones were specifically about British rule in India. This book became a great success, it was reprinted in 1820, 1826, and 1840 and the and it became a basic textbook for the British Indian Civil Service officers undergoing training at the East India Company's college at Haileybury. As the volumes covering the rise of British dominance in India followed the first three, James Mill's work began to considered an authoritative history of India. The six-volume edition of 1844, edited by H.H. Wilson contained notes by the editor pointing to errors and inadequacies in Mill's narrative. But the book continued to be considered a classic.

Mill's entire work was written on the basis of his limited readings in books and reports by European authors on India. It contained a good deal of the prejudice about India and the natives of India which many British officers acquired in course of their stay in India. However, despite shortcomings from the point of view of authenticity and veracity and objectivity, the book was very influential for two reasons. One of these reasons is often recognized: James Mill belonged to an influential school of political and economic thought, the Utilitarians inspired by the philosopher Jeremy Bentham. As a Utilitarian exposition of history Mill's history of India was also at the same time implicitly a Utilitarian agenda for British administration in India. Thus the book had far-reaching influence on British policies in India. The other reason for the immense influence the book exercised has not been recognized as much as one might have expected. This book perfectly reflected the cast of mind at the beginning of the nineteenth century which we have noticed earlier, a cast of mind which developed in the wake of Britain's victory in the Anglo-French wars for hegemony in Europe, and post-Industrial Revolution Britain's growing economic prosperity. James Mill broadcast a message of confident imperialism which was exactly what the readers in England wanted to hear.

The fact that Mill had never seen India, nor knew any of its languages, did not deter him. He thought that it was possible to 'obtain more knowledge of India in one year, in his closet in England, than he could obtain ... by the use of his eyes and ears in India.'[15] His reputation as the historian of India helped him advance in his career; after his initial appointment in the East India Company's headquarters in London in 1819, he rapidly rose to the high position of 'Chief Examiner' of correspondence, a position which allowed him a role in drafting policy making documents. In the meanwhile, the main lesson imparted by his history became a part of the received wisdom in England: that the civilization of India was never at a high level, that the Indian modes of governance and the laws and institutions were despicable, and that the 'Hindus have much to gain by a change of masters,'[16] that is, the coming of the British, the masters of the world.

While it will be pointless to provide here a blow by blow account of the treatment that 'Indian civilization' received from the successors to James Mill, popular historians of India mainly from the ranks of the Indian Civil Service, a quick survey of the major figures in that story may be useful. The historical work which rivalled Mill's work in terms of influence on the nineteenth century mind was produced by Mountstuart Elphinstone in 1841. There is a remarkable contrast between Mill who had no direct experience of India and Elphinstone who spent his entire working life from the age of sixteen years in India. He came out to India in 1795 as a writer, that is, junior-most civil servant, in the East India Company's service and by 1801 he had rapidly risen to the position of Assistant to the Company's Resident in the court of Peshwa Baji Rao; thereafter he made a natural transition to the position of British Resident in Nagpur (1804–8) and later at Pune (1811). He acquired immense diplomatic and social experience in interaction with Indian potentates and courts and at the same time he distinguished himself in action at the battles of Assaye and Argaon as well as the Third Maratha War of 1817–19. He retired as the Governor of Bombay Presidency and devoted himself to the task of writing a history of India.

While James Mill was known to have links with the Utilitarian school of thought—though it was his son John Stuart Mill who really contributed to the development of Utilitarianism as a political philosophy—Mountstuart Elphinstone is more difficult to categorize in terms of philosophical affiliation. Elphinstone, a civil servant in India for the greater part of his working life, was something of an empiricist and he was far better equipped and better informed than Mill to write a history of India. His work *History of Hindu and Muhammedan India* (1841) became a standard text in Indian universities (founded from 1857 onwards) and was reprinted up to the early years of the next century. Elphinstone followed this up with *History of British Power in the East*, a book that traced fairly systematically the expansion and consolidation of British rule till Hastings' administration.

When Elphinstone's *History of India* was published the discerning readership in England was aware of the shortcomings in James Mill's history of British India. A new edition of Mill's work in six volumes was edited by H.H. Wilson, the Boden Professor of Sanskrit at Oxford. Wilson courteously pointed to many errors in Mill's version of Indian history, especially pre-colonial history. However, the influence of Mill, at least on British historical imagination, seemed to remain intact, perhaps because the message in it was suited to the age of imperialism. It remained a text book in Haileybury College up to 1855. Elphinstone made no bones about the fact that Mill's opinions were questionable at times: as Elphinstone put it in his Preface, Mill's history 'left some room for doubt and discussion'. As regards Elphinstone's views on Indian civilization, it was closer to Sir William Jones's rather than James Mill's evaluation.

Hindus were once in a higher condition, both moral and intellectual, than they are now; and, as even in their present state of depression, they are on a footing of equality with any people out of Europe, it seems to follow that, at one time, they must have attained a state of civilisation only surpassed by a few of the most favoured of the nations, either of antiquity ... or of modern times.[17]

Words such as these must have been balm to the injured pride of the Indian readership. Moreover, due to his intimate knowledge of India, Elphinstone, bearing in mind things as he saw them in India, was able to arrive at a balanced judgement. He often compares historical events or institutions with his own personal experience as an observer. Chapters entitled 'Present State of Religion', 'Present State of Philosophy', and so on, contain Elphinstone's own observations of contemporary India, posited in a historical context.

While Elphinstone displays more sympathy with the Indian subjects under British rule, he remained the empire builder that he was in course of his career in the service of the East India Company. He looked upon the Mughals as predecessors of the British. His epitaph on the Mughal empire, by way of concluding remarks on the battle of Panipat of 1760 was abundantly clear. He comments that as the Mughal empire dies in 1760 'a new race of conquerors has already commenced its career, which may again unite the empire under better auspices than before.'[18]

A remarkable feature of Elphinstone's work was the awareness of the scale or size of the subcontinent he was writing about. He pays attention to regional history, the different trajectories of development in a manner not attempted before. In this *History of India* (1841), he first addresses in Books I to III the issue of the general state of Hindu or ancient Indian civilization. Then in Book IV he distinguished each region of 'Hindustan' and 'Dekkan' and attempts to chronicle their history. Books V to XII contained fairly detailed chronicles of the 'Mahometan Period'. Incidentally, the periodization of Indians history into ancient and medieval periods corresponding to 'Hindu' and 'Muslim' periods was henceforward established as a convention in Indian historiography. The consequent identification of the 'British' period with the 'modern' period was, of course, suited to the image of British rule as the harbinger of modernity.

A survey of the popular and influential Bitish historians of India in the nineteenth century will be incomplete if we do not include Sir Alfred Lyall. While Elphinstone's works continued to be influential as a textbook, especially in India, it was soon surpassed by Lyall's writings. He joined the Indian Civil Service in 1856, climbed his way up in the service to Lt-Governorship in the North-Western Provinces, and retired in 1887. He was in the Indian Civil Service at a time when racist attitudes had hardened under the impact of the Rebellion of 1857. And yet he showed an open-minded attitude to things Indian and published essays on Indian religions and philosophy in *Asiatic Studies,* published in two volumes in 1882 and 1899. But his major work *Rise and Expansion of British Dominion in India* (1894) was historical. The first version of this work was published in 1893 under the title 'Rise of the British Dominion in India'; within a year a third edition came out in 1894 with substantial expansion and that is when the title was changed to include the word 'Expansion', The edition of 1907 underwent further expansion to cover the period from 1857–1907. The book was a literary success of a sort and underwent several reprints.

In his interpretation of Indian history, Lyall used a very wide canvas, looking at the incursion of the British in India in the light of the relationship between the West and the East from the days of the Greeks and the Romans. This wide sweep of history, a wide-angled global view of relationship between civilizations, was different from that of most contemporary British historians of India. His history begins with an examination of the history of European nations as marine powers and the importance of seaborne trade. And he often refers to historical trends in Europe to understand what happened in the East. For instance he speculated that

...in England the tolerant and progressive ideas of the 18th century operated rather favourably than otherwise towards the spread of the Asian dominion. As commerce has invariably promoted freethinking in religion and politics all the world over, so rationalism and liberal principles in their turn helped commerce, by saving Englishmen from the mistakes and prejudices that had hampered the commercial enterprise of Spain, Portugal and partly of France....The calm and open temper of the English mind at this period (viz. 18th century) may be numbered among the moral conditions that were advantageous to the East India Company in contending for supremacy in India.[19]

The theory may be questioned, but such attempts to connect thought trends in Europe to the external events of wars and the quotidian trivia of the counting house were rare in British Indian historiography.

A notable element in Lyall's work was his theoretical position that India and Europe were on the same track of development, but India's development was arrested at a certain point. India as an 'arrested civilization' was an influential idea in Europe but in India it had few takers. The nationalistically inclined intelligentsia rejected the view that India was just a backward version of Europe; they believed that India was radically different from Europe in the organization of her society and state systems, and that India must be allowed to work out a different historical destiny rather than try to imitate Europe. At any rate, while in some matters Lyall's interpretative framework may be questioned, his attempt to look at India as a civilization merits recognition.[20]

Unlike the average British historian of India, Lyall touched upon many sensitive questions which they shirked. For instance, he noted that the British occupied all the important positions of decision making in colonial India, especially in the early days or during colonial rule. His explanation was that 'foreign domination must necessarily be more or less autocratic for some time after it has been acquired.' He compares the situation with the administration of the early Moghuls who mainly used 'men of their own race'.[21] Again, when talking about Macaulay's Minute on education in India, pouring ridicule on Indian knowledge systems and literature, Lyall is critical, unlike your average British civil servant of his times: 'Macaulay, with all his genius, lacked sympathy with the deeper and more delicate fibres of national sensitiveness.'[22] Or again, taking favourable notice of Bentinck, much admired in Indian intellectual circles at that time, Lyall remarks on the contrast between him and most other Governors-General of that period, known for their aggrandizing policies: Bentinck's administration was 'in Anglo-Indian history a period of *brief and rare* tranquility....of liberal and civilising administration.' [23]

However, with all his intellectual predispositions to get away from the mindset of the usual British civil servant in late nineteenth century India, Sir Alfred Lyall was true to his role as an 'empire builder'. He admired another great empire builder, Warren

Hastings, 'a man of highest character', and defended him against
critics like Edmund Burke. Hastings' 'integrity was virulently
aspersed, and all his public acts wantonly distrusted in speeches that
invoked against him the moral indignation of partisans engaged in
the ignoble wrangle over places, pensions and sinecures....'[24] Lyall
was convinced that British rule was beneficial to India. Around
fifty years after the Rebellion of 1857 he wrote: 'The moral and
material civilization of the Indian people has made more progress
in the last fifty years [he was writing in 1907] than during all the
preceding centuries of their history.'[25] He was also rather sceptical
of the Indian natives' 'desire for a larger share in the government of
their country.'[26]

On the whole, while the Indian readers perceived in James Mill's
history preconceived prejudices and plain ignorance, since Mill had
never been to India nor did he know any Indian language to access
sources, colonial historians of later times were undoubtedly better
informed. In Elphinstone or Lyall's writings one can see moments
of empathy with the civilization of a country where they had served
for the greater part of their life. At the same time one can see in
colonial historiography moments of assertion of another kind:
the colonial historians were the bearers of another civilization, a
hegemonic civilization, and the spokesmen of an imperial mission.
A clash became inevitable when historical consciousness found
expression in the writings of the first generation of Indians who
had undergone university education and had access to the English
language and British works of history. That was the generation of
Bankimchandra Chatterjee or R.G. Bhandarkar.

* * *

Bankimchandra Chatterjee graduated from the University of Calcutta
in 1858, the first to take a degree from an Indian university. His
contemporary R.G. Bhandarkar was one of the first four graduates
of the University of Bombay. Both were deeply interested in India's
past, Bhandarkar as one of the first professional historians of India
and Chatterjee as a litterateur. In order to understand the origins

of the discourse of civilization in modern India we may focus upon
these two representative figures among the products of 'modern
education' in nineteenth century India.

Before Bankimchandra appeared on the scene, there were some
anticipations of the Indian response to the Western critique of
Indian civilization. Among the students of Hindu college from 1817
and particularly from 1826 when Henry Louis Vivian Derozio
began to teach, there developed a new intellectual movement in
Calcutta. A group of young middle-class alumni of the college,
known as the 'Young Bengal' group, formed an association known
by the awkward but innocuous name, Society for the Acquisition of
General Knowledge and took up the task of responding to foreign
critics of Indian history and civilization. Consider, for instance, the
presentation made by Baboo Peary Chand Mitra at the meeting of
this association on 8 September 1841 on 'the State of Hindoostan
under the Hindoos.'[27] Mitra cites against James Mill's ill-informed
generalization about Hindoo institutions and laws, the authority
of H.H. Wilson (in his critical edition of Mill's *History of British
India*) and Mountstuart Elphinstone, as well as original documents
of the East India Company to contest the view that the monarch
in India possessed all the land, an error replicated from Francois
Bernier through James Mill to Karl Marx. Or consider Gobindra
Chandra Sen[28] writing about the history of India: 'In this country ...
we do not have any books narrating the events of history. But now
people want to know the history of our own native land and that
is why we urgently need today books on history.'[29] Mitra writes
on 14 September 1839: the ancient Hindus' history 'is defective,
are we therefore to declare that they have *no history?*...when we
peruse the first histories of all nations, says [David] Hume, we are
apt to imagine ourselves transported to some new world where the
whole frame of nature is disjointed....But that all proceeds from
usual propensity of mankind towards the marvelous....'[30] Thus we
see in the 1830s a hunger for history of a kind which would answer
the Western evaluation of India's civilization.

If this was a trend among the 'English educated' Indians, what of the traditional intellectuals, the pandits and *maulavis* and other bearers of traditional learning? Their role in the discovery of India's past is as yet an unexplored subject. From the research of Duncan Derrett, Jan Heesterman, P.V. Kane, Axel Michaels and others we know of the gradual erosion of the position of the pandit in colonial India.[31] Michaels has summed it up succinctly when he says that while in the Dharmashastra the pandit is a legal adviser with high authority, and in *Sukraniti* and nineteenth century Maharashtra he was a minister with both authority and power, in the East India Company's regime, after an initial spell of authority as the interpreter of Hindu law, the pandit loses his position when the codification of Hindu law was completed under British auspices. As regards the pandit's scholarship, it was recognized as a resource to be used, but the pandit and maulavi were treated at best as informants, not as intellectual colleagues to be acknowledged.[32] The role of pandits serving English Orientalists was considerable in deciphering texts and inscriptions and translation. Their names are to be found in the proceedings of the Asiatic Society of Calcutta: Radhakanta Sharma, Ramlochan, Sabar Tiwari, Ramdas Sen, Mathura Nath, Madhav Rao, Ramgovinda, Kamalakanta, Govinda Shastri. But in the papers authored and published by English scholars their contribution was seldom acknowledged.[33] Madhav M. Deshpande in an interesting study of the 'evolution of pandits into professors' in nineteenth century Maharashtra points to the departure R.G. Bhandarkar made from traditional Sanskritic modes of thought in the direction of modern critical scholarship.[34] It was the generation of Bhandarkar and Bankimchandra Chatterjee who acquired familiarity with and application of methods of modern critical scholarship, distinct from the methods with which the traditional intellectuals were identified.

Bankimchandra Chatterjee's literary career began in 1865 when he published his first novel, *Durgesh-nandini*. It is commonly accepted that in no Indian language at that time was the novel as a genre known, yet. (A contemporary of Bankimchandra, O.

Chandu Menon published the novel, *Indulekha*, in Malayalam in 1889.) Bankimchandra was not only the author of the first novel in the Bengali language, but also the founder and editor of the first literary journal in Bengali.[35] While he was the editor, from 1872–6, he published in this journal, *Banga-darshana*, a fairly large corpus of essays on various subjects including the theme of 'civilization' in India. He used the term *sabhyata* as a synonym for civilization, a term derived from classical Sanskrit literature; in *Raghuvansa* the great poet Kalidasa (*c.* fifth century AD) had used the word *sabhya* to suggest a level of culture appropriate to those who were fit to be a part of the *sabha*, or an assembly of cultivated persons.[36] The term was already current in Bengali language since Michael Madhusudan Dutt, one of the leading figures of the early Renaissance in Bengal, had used that term as a synonym for 'civilization' (for example, in a play written by him, 'Is This *Sabhyata*?'). Bankim invented a term for 'culture', *anushilana*, but this term did not find favour with his contemporaries and the synonym which was widely accepted later was '*sanskriti*'.[37] The fact that Bankim had to resort to neologism suggests that although he and his contemporaries were part of an old civilization, the theme of civilization was being addressed afresh in the discourse of the modern intellectuals.

In his early writings Bankim offers a theory about civilization, particularly Indian civilization. He expounds these views first in 1872, in the journal he edited in an essay entitled 'The Law of Nature'—a part of a series of essays on the condition of the lower orders in Bengal.[38] Bankim theorizes that natural environment is the crucial determinant of the origin and progress of civilization. Civilizations developed in the world in countries where the soil was fertile enough to generate a surplus. Such a surplus was needed to make it possible for at least a part of the population to engage in the pursuit of knowledge. 'Some countries produce a social surplus, some do not. Where there is such surplus, civilization develops. When there is none, the country fails to develop a civilization.'[39] The precondition is that 'surplus should exceed what is needed to sustain the labouring classes.' India was fortunate in its abundant natural resources and hence was able to develop a civilization very early on. However, while this precondition was satisfied, the further advance of civilization was hampered by some basic flaws in the civilization that developed. First, society came to be divided into two parts: the labouring classes, and at the other end a small class living on surplus without engaging in labour to produce that surplus. To this latter class belonged the Brahmins, and more generally speaking all those who depended solely on their mental faculties (*buddhi-upajeebee*). In course of time 'the power of the latter over the labouring classes increased. A result of that was greater exploitation. That power is at the root of the anti-Shudra prescriptions of the *smriti* [Hindu law] texts.'[40] The end product was 'the poverty, ignorance, slavery' of the majority of people.

Bankim goes on to say that in countries like India there was also a natural factor which slowed down or hampered the advancement of civilization. We can perhaps say that what he says here amounts to a paradox. On the one hand fertile soil and clement climate aided the early origination of civilization. On the other hand the same environmental conditions retarded further development because those conditions made it easy to earn a living; exertion was unnecessary, and aspiration for higher levels of living was less strong than it was in colder climates and hostile environments. It was natural for people to be content under the circumstances. And such contentment was counterproductive, it did not push men towards progress.

Some of Bankim's ideas are close to those of H.T. Buckle (1821–1862) in his *History of Civilization in England*.[41] Indeed Bankim cites him as an authority on the subject of Nature as a determinant of growth of civilizations, though his observations about India were mostly his own.[42] Bankim was also influenced by William E.H. Lecky (1838–1903) who had argued in his book, *The Rise of Rationalism in Europe* (1865), that desire for material betterment was a factor in advancing rational knowledge and the study of the natural sciences. Bankim finds such a drive for material betterment wanting in Indian culture. In its place there was contentment and that was held up as an ideal in prevailing ideology. 'Whether it is the Brahmins or the Buddhists, Hindu lawgivers or philosophers, all of them have taught Indians that material goods are worthless. Thus religious teachings have reinforced nature-ordained contentment.'[43]

This exposition of the history of civilization was remarkable not only for its attention to a materialist explication of the history of civilization. Equally remarkable is the critique of Brahminical hegemony in India's civilization. 'The Brahmins cast a net of Shastric [scriptural] and prescriptive injunctions to imprison the *kshatriyas, vaishyas* and *shudras*....There was no end to their [Brahmin-made] rules. From the rules concerning the system of justice and governance in peace and war, to every action in daily life, everything was regulated by brahminic precepts....The net in which they ensnared India eventually trapped the Brahmins too.'[44] They began to forget how to exercise their mind because they became slaves of blind habit created by their own prescriptions. In a later essay entitled 'Equality' (*Samya*) published in 1863 Bankim compared Indian and European civilizations. In medieval Europe, as in India in ancient times, the Church and the priests taught the people to spurn this world and material betterment. But the Renaissance, Bankim goes on to say, broke the spell of priestly influence. 'The rejection of worldly pursuits was given up. Thereafter civilization progressed. Thus in Europe that tendency of mind was not permanently implanted. But in India this mentality has become second nature amongst our people.' Hence there was a difference between Europe re-awakened and India. The result of the pursuit of material betterment and the efforts of the lower orders in Europe for self-improvement produced 'a good life, wealth, advance of civilization.'[45] This forthright attack on the Brahminic order was written by Bankim in 1872–3, when he was young (he was thirty-five years of age and relatively junior in his service to the British Indian government). Later in life Bankim was more cautious and used to say that in writing this essay in 1873 he had been much influenced by John Stuart Mill's ideas; in later editions he began to insert a note that his ideas had undergone a change since 1873.[46]

However, in respect of his ideas about Brahminism in Indian civilization, Mill's writings were not relevant. Independent of that, young Bankim arrived at a stern critique of the role of Brahminism in Indian civilization.

In his old age, in the last ten years of his life till his death in 1894, Bankim wrote a number of thick tomes on religion, including a commentary on the *Geeta* (the subject of many other nineteenth century intellectuals like K.T. Telang and Balagangadhar Tilak).[47] In these later writings Bankim was milder in his criticism of Brahminism. However he continued to maintain an attitude to religion which was informed with an anthropological approach in some ways. He often cited a leading contemporary anthropologist, Tylor. Sir Edward Burnett Tylor (1832–1917), professor of anthropology at Oxford, was the author of two widely read works, *Researches into the Early History of Mankind* (1865) and *Primitive Culture* (1871). Bankim quotes passages from the latter and it seems that he was also familiar with the other one.[48] His approach to religion, for example, in *Krishna-charitra* (1886, 1892) and his essays on Hindu deities (*Deva-tattwa*, comprising essays written in the 1880s), came close Edward Tylor's, 'The origin of religion is a matter of scientific investigation', he writes in *Dharma-tattwa*, 1888.[49] 'Our research must follow scientific method....It is best to study the religious beliefs of the primitive people to understand the origins of religion.' Perhaps we can see the influence of European anthropologists' approach in Bankim's adoption of the concepts 'primitive' (*adim*) and 'uncivilized' (*asabhya*).[50] The idea of 'the primitive' was to figure prominently in the anthropological discourse in respect of tribal people in India in late colonial times—but that was in the early twentieth century, long after Bankim's death.

We may now turn from Bankimchandra's notions about religion as an element in civilization to another question which engaged him. How did he situate India's civilization vis-à-vis that of the West? On this issue Bankim's thinking was deeply infused with a consciousness of India's dependent status under British rule. Why did India lose independence, was India confronted with a superior civilization, was India a nation, how to unite the different 'races' in India, was the evolution of an European style 'patriotism' or 'nationalism' a desirable end for India? Such were the questions he addressed time and again.

To begin with, we might note that the innate tendency of Bankim's writings is to represent the British in India not so much as the bearers of Western culture and civilization, but as the conquerors of India. He acknowledged British supremacy and, like his contemporary R.G. Bhandarkar, Bankim generally refrains from asserting the superiority of India's civilization compared to Western civilization. At the same time, he was emphatic in rejecting European scholars' adverse evaluation of Indian civilization. He made fun of their ignorance of classical Sanskrit and of their habit of giving credence to the slightest evidence from foreign sources rather than indigenous sources.[51] Bankim was somewhat obsessed with the glorious heritage of India's ancient past. While acknowledging his indebtedness to John Stuart Mill, Auguste Comte, H.T. Buckle, or Herbert Spencer, he was highly sceptical of the European Sanskritists and Indologists. Some of those authors he thought were contemptuous of India, for example, Albrecht Weber (1825–1901); some of them Bankim condemned as linguistically ill-equipped to use the sources in Sanskrit, for instance, J. Talboys Wheeler (1824–1897); and some others were pedants who were learned but had no access to what Bankim believed to be the inner meanings of works in Sanskrit. For a few scholars such as the German Indologist Theodor Goldstucker (1821–1872) he had genuine regard.[52]

Bankim was deeply impressed with the social and political virtues of the European civilization. In 1873 Bankim writes that generally speaking, compared to the people of the country, it will be conceded by any person who is not blinded by racial prejudice, that the English were

...superior in terms of power, culture, knowledge, and prestige. An individual in Bengal may be superior to an individual in England, but if you look at the average, the Englishman is superior....Therefore if, as inferiors we are not submissive, obedient, servile and devoted, they do not like it....

The English are conquerors, we are the conquered ones. But it is not in human nature that the conquered will be devoted to the conqueror, nor is it natural for the conqueror not to display his superior power. We are no doubt obedient servants, but we can not be submissively devoted. Obedience may be on our lips, but not in our hearts.[53]

Thus he wrote in 'Jati Baira' (Racial Animosity), published in 1873. Bankim went on to say that the outcome of this relationship was mutual racial animosity but that was not an undesirable thing. 'We pray earnestly that until the day when we are equal to the English racial animosity will remain alive....On account of racial animosity we are trying to compete with them.'[54] Bankim concludes that all efforts on the part of newspapers and political associations and the like to reduce racial animosity were not only destined to fail but these efforts were not necessarily good for Indians under British rule, for they must not forget their subjection under that rule.

Bankim attributed the progress made by European civilization to the advancement of knowledge, especially science. He writes in 1872: 'it is their science which has empowered Europeans to conquer the world....Some people believe that brute force alone enabled Europeans to establish this supremacy in India but actually it is no exaggeration to say that European supremacy was due to their mastery over science and that is also their means of preserving their supremacy.'[55] On the other hand the scientific knowledge which India had developed at one time in astronomy, algebra, geometry, mathematics, botany and medicine, musicology, inductive logic, etc. was gradually forgotten. Scientific and technological superiority allowed Britain to monopolize the textile market where India was once supreme. (While Bankim rues the neglect of science in India in his times, he also noted that there were exceptions, for instance, the mathematician Ram Chandra of Delhi College, or Mahendra Lal Sarkar in medicine.) One can connect Bankim's observation on the decline of science in India with his views on the degeneration of the Brahmins which we have noted earlier.

Next to the European cultivation of science, the other attribute that Bankim identified as the cause of European supremacy was the growth of nationalism in modern Europe. He refers to the unification of Germany and Italy in his own life time and laments the absence of that national spirit in his own country.[56]

There are many nationalities [*jati*] in India. Given the differences in their habitation environment, their language, their racial characteristics, their religious beliefs, they are indeed different. The Bengali, the Punjabi, the Troilangis [people of Telengana], the Marathis, the Rajputs, the Jaths, the Hindus, the Muslims, who will unite with whom? Where there is religious unity there is none in terms of racial affinity, when there is racial affinity there is none in languages used, when there is linguistic unity there is separation in terms of territory....Not only that. Fate has ordained that in India even when there is unity in terms of religion, language, race, territorial integrity, despite all bonds of unity there is no consciousness of unity....If many nationalities are subjected to a common imperial rule, the subjected people lose their consciousness of nationality....They lose some of their distinctive characteristics, but they do not gain a sense of unity. This happened to the constituent races of the Holy Roman Empire. This has happened to the Hindus as well. For all these reasons, India never witnessed the establishment of a truly national entity. Because it never happened, the Hindus have never raised a finger to defend their independence.

There were only a few instances of an approach towards nation building [*jati pratishtha*]. Two such instances, according to him were to be seen in Shivaji's Maharashtra and Ranjit Singh's Khalsa. Bankim examined the multifaceted Indian civilization in the past and could not find any evidence of a national aspiration for independence. That was not a part of India's tradition and culture. In Sanskrit or in Bengali language there was not even an exact equivalent to the concept of a 'nation'. The efforts of Shivaji and Ranjit Singh were rare instances in the long history of the Hindu community. Bankim considered in this context only the Hindu community, excluding the Muslims, and concluded that nationalism in the proper sense of the term 'was unknown to the Hindus'.[57] These were his observations in an essay published in the journal he edited, *Banga Darshana* in 1872.

Bankim pushes the argument further to say that even in classical Sanskrit texts it is difficult to find any endorsement of the idea of political independence. 'The Kings tried to keep their kingdom,

the brave displayed their bravery, the warrior caste fought hard....
But the aspiration for independence was not a natural thing to the
common people.'[58] Where are the instances of 'the common people
[*sadharana janagana*] enthused and actively fighting, inspired by
the idea that we do not want an alien ruler?'[59] When Hindu rulers
fell in battle 'no one else took the lead to defend independence from
amongst the general populace, there was no initiative to defend
the kingdom....And this was because of lack of unity within Hindu
society, the fact that nation formation did not occur in that society,
the absence of a spirit of service to the country, or whatever you
say.' In Europe the trend had been the opposite. 'Nation formation
is the ruling spirit; it has led to revolutionary changes. That is what
has unified Italy. That is what accounts for the establishment of the
new and mighty German empire.'[60] Bankimchandra concludes that
Europe offers two significant contributions: the ideal of independence
and object lessons in nation formation.[61] Incidentally Bankim raises
in another accompanying essay a significant question. Was the
status of the lower castes any better before India's subjection to
British rule? His answer was that their subjection to the rule of the
Brahmins and Kshatriyas had been such that political independence
or dependence made little difference to them.[62] The implication is
that caste division impedes unity to attain independence. But he
does not elaborate on this point.

On the whole the originality in Bankim's observation was, first,
to distinguish between the holders of state power and the common
people, and thus to distinguish between the royal desire to preserve a
kingdom and the common people's urge for independence. Second,
he also differentiated between the lower and higher strata of people
to argue that the loss of political independence meant very little in
terms of the existential conditions of the lower strata.

Two further points need to be made. First, a change in his
attitude in the later part of his life—while Bankim in his early
writings held up European nationalism as an ideal, in his later
writings he was critical of European nationalism and patriotism. 'In
Europe patriotism is a religion which enjoins the patriot to rob all

other nations to enrich one's own....It is this patriotism which has
led to the extermination of all the original inhabitants of America.
It is to be hoped that God will not ordain such a patriotic future
for Indians.'[63] Bankim proposed for India a universalist ideal which
included love for one's kins, love for the country (*swadesh priti*)
and a friendly regard for the world as a whole. It was desirable
to strike a balance between all these elements. Such a balance was
conspicuously absent in India. Love for the country, he surmised,
was generally inconsequential for Indians. Thus Bankimchandra,
the progenitor of an intense patriotism, found India of the past—he
had in mind a Hindu *Bharatavarsha*—wanting in that respect.

The second feature of Bankimchandra's writings is that he
created, so to speak, a language to address some of the issues
discussed above. We have seen earlier that he puzzled over the
question of the accurate synonyms for 'civilization' and 'culture.'
His problem was more acute when he sought in Bengali language
the word for 'nation.' The word that came to his mind was *jati* and
he writes:

The word *jati* has many meanings. First, Caste in Hindu society, e.g.
Brahmin, Kayastha, Koibarta [one of the lower castes in Bengal]. Second,
jati means Nation in the sense of people in a particular country; e.g. the
English, the French, the Chinese. Third, *jati* means Race; e.g. the Aryans,
the Semetics, the Turanis, etc. Fourth, *jati* means Tribe, a category of
people in some countries; e.g. the Jews had ten tribes among them. Fifth,
jati means Species [of animals]....In the Bengali language there is no word
other than *jati* to convey all these different meanings.[64]

Chatterjee was compelled to write in an early essay the simplest of
definitions; he writes in 1872: 'In this essay the term *Jati* connotes
Nation or Nationality.'[65] Similar problems must have been observed
in other linguistic regions of India in Bankimchandra's times. In an
encounter between civilizations concepts travel across borders and
language accommodates new words and meanings.

To sum up Bankimchandra Chatterjee's approach to the issue
of civilization in India and in Europe is not easy. However, despite

some changes his ideas underwent in his old age, some ideas re-
curred. First, he had a theory of Nature being a determinant of
the rise and progress of civilizations. This view was similar to that
expounded by H.T. Buckle. Second, he considered religious beliefs a
major element in civilizations. He adopted, inspired by the writings
of Edward Tylor, an anthropological approach to the sociology of
religion. In his early writings he was critical of Brahminical hegemony but this critique was muted in his later writings. Third, he
recognized the British not so much as the bearers of the European
civilization in India, but as the conquerors of India. Indians, he
wrote, must not forget that they were a subjected race. And finally,
he was a great admirer of the scientific advances made in Europe as
well as of the social and political qualities of the British, in particular their national spirit; these were the attributes of the civilization
of the conquerors, he thought, and these were the areas where India
in modern times was backward. That dissatisfaction with the distance between two civilizations, that injured self-esteem eventually
gave rise to an intense patriotism which found expression in the
song 'Vande Mataram' which was to become after Independence
one of the two national songs of the Indian Republic.

* * *

While Bankimchandra Chatterjee was the first graduate of an
Indian university and one of the first two graduates of the Calcutta
University, R.G. Bhandarkar was one of the first four graduates
of Bombay University. Bankimchandra was a civil servant and a
littérateur without specialization in history, while Bhandarkar can
be regarded as one of the first professional historians in nineteenth
century India. Bhandarkar's publications, as Prachi Deshpande
points out, marked a departure from the earlier tradition of Sanskrit
pundits in going beyond Sanskritic learning to critical construction
of chronology and dynastic histories, with special attention
to 'authentic' sources, particularly numismatic and epigraphic
sources.[66] Given this orientation, his explicit engagement with

the discourse of civilization was not very deep. Yet his sustained scholarly work over decades was far from being irrelevant to that discourse.

An apposite example is the fact that the very basis of the claim made by Tagore or Gandhi about the absorption of so-called foreigners into the social fabric of Indian civilization was provided by Bhandarkar—and, of course, by a host of European scholars in the late nineteenth century. In 1909 Bhandarkar sums up his seminal research on this in an essay, 'The Incorporation of Pre-Mahomedan Foreigners into the Hindu Social Organisation'. He points out a huge number of inscriptions ranging from laudatory inscriptions about royal dynasties to votive inscriptions by common people in Hindu and Buddhist sacred sites to show how the Indo-Greeks or Yavanas, Sakas, Abhiras, Turushkas, Magas, Hunas, and the Gujars who came into India were absorbed into Hindu society.[67] G.K. Gokhale who happened to be a young member of the Deccan Sabha audience (he was younger to Bhandarkar by thirty years), at once sensed the significance of these data; the text of the lecture was prepared by Bhandarkar at the request of Gokhale. To put to an end a myth current in his times Bhandarkar observed: 'The foreigners who came to India before the Mohamedans were absorbed so quickly and on such a large scale in Hindu social organization, that in modern society any attempt to decide who is Aryan and who a non-Aryan would be quite futile.'[68] He endorsed the exhortation of G.K. Gokhale that 'we must also mix with' the Mohamedans who were not absorbed in the same manner as other immigrants earlier. Bhandarkar's research on the absorption of 'foreign' ethnic groups was the kind of historical research that provided the stuff and substance of the theory of a syncretic civilization which nationalist public spokesmen constructed later.

At the same time, Bhandarkar refused to be a part of the nationalist chorus of praise for ancient Indian civilization. He believed that 'advancement of the individual was the object of thought and endeavour with the Hindus' and that

India has lived an individual life not a corporate or national life....Hindus
had in all likelihood, no conception of a national existence, and therefore
did not concern themselves with questions about the national weal. We
have an extensive religious, poetical, and legendary literature, but no
work on politics or history....The effect of this indifference to corporate or
national interests was that, from time to time, the country was governed by
foreigners....But now, with our minds enlightened by our contact with the
Western nationals, we cannot afford to be indifferent to our national and
corporate interests.[69]

The recognition of the value of contact with the West recurs very
frequently in Bhandarkar's writings. We have cited above what he
wrote in 1902. Earlier, in 1888, he wrote of the West: there he sees
'a whole civilisation, which undoubtedly is far superior to ours
in a great many points', particularly in respect of 'the principle
of progress [which] is very strong in their civilisation.'[70] Or again
in 1894, his Convocation Address as Vice Chancellor, Bombay
University:

A wise Indian patriot will take pride in the fact that this country forms a
very important member of the Empire over which the sun never sets, and
that India is one of the brightest jewels, if not the brightest, in the British
crown....[England] has consciously undertaken the function of civilizing
India, and this University is one of the many evidences available. She has
given us an orderly and stable government....[Bhandarkar mentions here
thuggees, pindaris, right to property, railways, telegraph, postal system,
and so on] We may even ask for powers and privileges. But before we do so
we should take care to qualify ourselves for their exercise.[71]

Bhandarkar went on to say that he was speaking at a 'momentous
period of the history of India', for that was a time when 'the
intellect and the moral sense of our country must wake up under
the influence of European civilisation'. That was a necessity because
Indian civilizations had undergone degeneration. Indians must 'look
back upon the history of our race [to] trace with an unbiased mind
its progress towards civilisation and observe the phenomenon of its
stagnancy, or more truly, its decline and degradation'.[72]

These extracts represent a strand of thinking which was to be
found in some contemporary writings in Calcutta, Madras or

Bombay along with the more nationalistic strand which Gandhi represented. An interesting confrontation between these two lines of thinking occurred when M.G. Ranade criticized, at a meeting of the Bombay Graduates' Association, Bhandarkar's Convocation Address quoted above. Basically Ranade's point was that a more positive evaluation of the Indian scene than Bhandarkar's was possible. Bhandarkar's reply to this criticism fudged the main issue and focused on minor debating points.

To give credit where it is due, Bhandarkar in his other writings delivers a more qualified judgement on the state of Indian civilization or the merits of European civilization. For instance, in 1893, while saying that in colleges like the Deccan College 'we are introduced to a civilization....greatly different from our own', he says that the task for the educated Indian is to compare the two civilizations to form a judgement.[73] A 'wholesale adoption' of Western civilization 'argues a shallowness of mind', and again 'to suppose and to declare, out of mistaken pride, that everything we have is good is pernicious.' Civilizations must learn from one another was his message.[74] Bhandarkar was forced to take a stance on the civilizational question for two reasons. One is related to the state of his discipline: he rejected the false pride which led some Indian scholars to praise Indian heritage without regard to evidence and historical method. Second, he was a sincere believer in the need for social reform in India and this led him to make very critical remarks which some patriotic natives found offensive.

Bhandarkar was often highly critical of Indian scholars and sometimes of European scholars in the field of early Indian history. Of Indian scholarship his chief complaint was the absence of a critical comparative method to build a history which would be a 'record of events as they occurred'—a phrase that reminds one of Leopold von Ranke. He roundly condemned 'the most uncritical spirit that has come over us of praising ourselves and our ancestors indiscriminately' instead of trying to 'critically and impartially examine our old records and institutions.'[75] These observations made in 1888 were replicated thirty years later in his inaugural address at the Bhandarkar Oriental Research Institute in 1918 when he again spoke of 'the temptations of an Indian scholar' to discover the imagined anticipation of European inventions old Indian texts in supposed 'allusion to the x-ray, railways, and what not.'[76] Critical Indian scholarship alone he said would 'put an end to the disparaging tone which European scholars speak of us....' He became acquainted with some European scholars during his visit to Europe in the middle of his life to attend the Orientalist Congress. With some of these scholars these meetings were too brief to be of any value. There was, for instance, the famous classical scholar Benjamin Jowett of Balliol College. This was the self-important man about whom fellow-students of Lord Curzon at Balliol College wrote a rhyme: 'I am Benjamin Jowett/Master of Balliol College/All that is knowledge I know it/ What I don't know isn't knowledge.' Bhandarkar writes that there was scarcely any conversation between him and Jowett. But he did not feel slighted. One may surmise that it was almost as if Bhandarkar visited a monument.

As regards European scholarship in general, Bhandarkar's admiration was obvious, but that did not restrain his criticism of many individual scholars. Most notable among these writings is his review of the eminent historian Vincent Smith's *Early History of India* in 1909. Bhandarkar points out many differences between Smith's and his own account in his *Peep into Early History of India* and *Early History of the Deccan*. To his judgement, Vincent Smith's book was good in parts but sometimes failed to produce authentic evidence; it appears to be the natural reaction of a scholar who prefers to refrain from adopting a kind of general perspective excluding local particularities which a comprehensive history of early India demanded. Bhandarkar criticized many European scholars but he undoubtedly gave greater weightage to European scholarship in general.

Bhandarkar's approach to the past and present of Indian society and culture is of importance from the point of the discursive tradition we are concerned with. When one goes through the entire corpus of his writings one can see the enormous range of the questions he raised. In the Presidential Address to Bombay Provincial Social Conference in 1902 he raised questions uncomfortable to blind admirers of Indian culture.[77] Why are there 'separate clubs of Brahman Saraswats, or Senvis, Chandraseniya Kayasthas, and Daivajnas?' Why do the Marathas and Brahmans fight in Kolhapur over the question whether Rajas of Kolhapur and Baroda were Kshatriyas? Why did Iswarchandra Vidyasagar despair of social reform and why 'in Bengal social reform is almost given up' by all, except for the Brahmo Samaj? Why was the number of castes increasing over time 'unchecked by national considerations'? If the Japanese can bring about social modernization in the three decades since the Meiji Restoration, why is Indian social reform so slow? Bhandarkar writes in 1894, in reply to Ranade's critique mentioned earlier: 'what I have been doing during the last seven or eight years is to call attention to the defects and shortcomings of my countrymen....[because] without a reform of our social institution real political advance is impossible.'[78]

This trend of thinking was regarded by nationalist politicians as tantamount to apostasy. When Bhandarkar was nominated by the Government of Bombay to the Imperial Legislative Council, he indeed played a conservative role, to the dismay of nationalist leaders. In the Imperial Council most Indian members like G.K. Gokhale or Sir Asutosh Mookerjee opposed the Indian Universities Bill of 1904 on the ground that politically motivated persons should be removed from the Senate. 'I may state generally that I entirely disagree with what has fallen from my Hon'ble friend Mr. Gokhale ... I must deprecate the turn that has been given [by opponents of the Bill] to this question as if it involved a conflict of interest between Natives and Europeans.' Bhandarkar believed that since 'the object of the university is....To instill European ideas in our minds' it followed that 'this can best be done by Europeans, I mean of course competent Europeans.' The latter were 'the apostles of *a higher and progressive civilization* who have come out to rouse the mind and conscience of India....' This is just one of the many examples of how varied discursive factors influenced discussions about civilization and how it spilled over to the distant terrains of debate.[79]

NOTES

1. Michael S. Dodson, *Orientalism, Empire and National Culture: India 1770–1880* (Cambridge University Press, Delhi, 2010); T. Ballantyne, *Orientalism and Race: Aryanism in the British Empire* (Palgrave, Basingstoke, 2002); B.S. Cohn, *Colonialism and Forms of Knowledge: The British in India* (Princeton University Press, Princeton, 1996); O.P. Kejariwal, *The Asiatic Society of Bengal and the Discovery of India's Past: 1784–1838* (Oxford University Press, New Delhi, 1988); D. Kopf, *British Orientalism and the Indian Renaissance* (Berkeley, 1969); J. Majeed, *Ungoverned Imaginings: James Mill's* The History of British India and Orientalism (Clarendon Press, Oxford, 1992); A. Michaels (ed.), *The Pandit: Traditional Scholarship in India* (New Delhi, Manohar, 2001).

2. Dodson, *Orientalism, Empire and National Culture*; P.B. Wagoner, 'Pre-colonial Intellectuals and the production of Colonial Knowledge', *Comparative Studies in Society and History*, vol. 45, no. 4, 2003, pp. 783–814; Gyan Prakash, '*Orientalism* Now', *History and Theory*, vol. 34, no. 3, 1995, pp. 199–212; Rosalind O'Hanlon and David Washbrook, 'After Orientalism: Culture, Criticism and Politics in the Third World', *Comparative Studies in Society and History*, vol. 34, no. 1, 1992, pp. 141–84; Gyan Prakash, 'Writing Post-Orientalist Histories of the Third World', *Comparative Studies in Society and History*, vol. 32, no. 2, 1990, pp. 383–408; these and other writings on the subject are discussed in Chapter Five in this book along with the impact of Edward Said, *Orientalism* (Pantheon Books, London, 1978).

3. Mill, *The History of British India* (Baldwin, Cradock, and Joy, London, 1817).

4. William Jones, 'Preface', *Sakuntalam* (in translation), cited by James Mill, *History of British India* (London, 1844; reprint New Delhi, 1972) , vol. I, p. 370.

5. James Mill, *History of British India*, vol. I, p. 458.

6. Ibid., p. 460.

7. Ibid., p. 461.

8. Ibid., p. 389.

9. Ibid., p. 373.

10. Ibid., p. 458.

11. Ibid., p. 469.

12. Ibid., p. 461.

13. Ibid., p. 456.

14. Ibid., preface to vol. I, p. 3.

15. Ibid., p. 7.

16. Ibid., p. 709.

17. Mounstuart Elphinstone, *The History of India* (London, 1841; reprint Allahabad, 1966), p. 202; this work was followed by his *Rise of British Power in the East* (London, 1887).

18. Elphinstone, *The History of India* (London, 1841, reprint Allahanad, 1966), p. 665.

19. Alfred C. Lyall, *The Rise and Expansion of British Dominion in India* (London, 1911, 5th ed.), p. 120.

20. Sabyasachi Bhattacharya, 'Paradigms Lost: Notes on Social History in India', *Economic and Political Weekly*, vol. XVIII, nos 14–15, 1982, pp. 692–8.

21. Lyall, *The Rise and Expansion of British Dominion in India*, p. 387.

22. Ibid., p. 311.

23. Ibid., p. 310.

24. Ibid., p. 216.

25. Ibid., p. 388.

26. Ibid., p. 387.

27. Gautam Chattopadhyay, *Awakening in Bengal in Early 19th Century: Selected Documents* (Progressive Publishers, Calcutta, 1965), pp. 246–62.

28. Ibid., pp. 198–239, circa 1840.

29. Ibid., p. 198.

30. Ibid., p. 132.

31. P.V. Kane, *History of the Dharmasastras* (BORS, Poona, vols. II and III, 1973, 1974); Duncan M. Derrett, *Religions, Law and Institutions in India* (Faber, London, 1968), pp. 225–73; Jan C. Heesterman, *The Inner Conflict of Tradition* (Chicago University Press, Chicago, 1985), pp. 26–44; Axel Michaels, 'Pandit as a Legal Adviser', in Axel Michaels (ed.), *The Pandit: Traditional Scholarship in India* (Manohar, Delhi, 2001, pp. 61–75).

32. O.P. Kejariwal, *Asiatic Society of Bengal and the Discovery of India: 1784–1838* (Oxford University Press, Delhi, 1988).

33. Ibid., pp. 51, 56, 71, 125, 129, 165, 170, 186, 204, 213.

34. M.M. Deshpande, 'Pandits and Professors: Transformation in the 19th Century Maharashtra', in Michaels (ed.), *The Pandit*, p. 135.

35. Amitra Sudan Bhattacharya, *Bankimchandra Jibani* (Bankimchandra: A Biography) (Ananda Publishers, Calcutta, 1991), p. 791.

36. 'Anukaran' (Imitation) (1872) in J.C. Bagal (ed.), *Bankim Rachanavali* (*BR* hereafter) (Sahitya Samsad, Calcutta, 1954) vol. II, p. 203 (unless stated otherwise the translations are mine).

37. *Dharma Tattwa* (Theory of Religion) (1884–5) in *Bankim Rachanavali*, vol. II, p. 585.

38. 'Prakritir Niyam' (Law of Nature), *Banga Deshe Krishak*, (1872), in *BR*, vol. II, p. 299.

39. Ibid., pp. 299–300.

40. 'Samya' (Equality), serialized 1872–3, published as a book in 1879. See *BR*, vol. II, pp. 301, 396.

41. H.T. Buckle, *History of Civilization in England*, 2 vols (London, J.W. Parker & Son, 1857–61).

42. 'Prakritir Niyam' (Law of Nature), in *BR*, vol. II, pp. 299, 302.

43. Ibid., pp. 302–3.

44. Ibid., pp. 303–4.

45. 'Samya', *BR*, vol. II, p. 397, cites H.T. Lecky.

46. Sris Chandra Majumder, *Bankim Prasanga*, cited in J.C. Bagal, 'Editor's Introduction', in *BR*, vol. II, p. XXXI.

47. Srimad-Bhagabat-Gita (serially published, 1886–8; posthumously published book, 1902), *BR*, vol. II, pp. 680–775; Bankim quotes K.T. Telang profusely, along with Sridhara and, of course, Shankaracharya, pp. 736, 774.

48. *Deva Tattwa, Hindu Dharma* (Hindu Deities and Religion) (1938), published posthumously, *BR*, vol. II, p. 790.

49. '*Dharma Tattwa*, *BR*, vol. II, p. 806.

50. 'Anukaran'(1872), *BR*, vol. II, p. 203.

51. *Krishna-Charitra* [Krishna Characterized] (1886, 1892), Chapter IV, *BR*, Vol. II, p. 413.

52. Ibid., pp. 420–2.

53. 'Jati-Baira'[Racial Animosity] (1873), *BR*, vol. II, p. 884.

54. Ibid.

55. 'Bharatvarshiya Vijnan Sabha' (Indian Association for Science) (1872), *BR*, vol. II, pp. 1024–8.

56. 'Bharat Kalanka' (India's Disgrace), *BR*, vol. II, p. 240.

57. Ibid., p. 241.

58. Ibid., p. 238.

59. Ibid., pp. 238–9.

60. Ibid., p. 239.

61. 'Bharater Swadhinata Paradhinata' (India's Independence and Subjection), *BR*, p. 241.

62. Ibid., pp. 244–5.

63. 'Swadesh Priti' (Love for the Country), '*Dharma Tattwa*, chapter 24, *BR*, vol. II, p. 661.

64. 'Artha Vyakti' (Connotation), *Pathya Pustak*, in *BR*, vol. II, p. 935.

65. 'Bharater Swadhinata evam Paradhinata', *BR*, vol. II, p. 241.

66. Prachi Deshpande, *Creative Pasts: Historical Memory & Identity in Western India, 1700–1788* (Permanent Black, Delhi, 2007), pp. 98–9.

67. V.G. Paranjape and N.B. Utgikar (eds), *Collected Works of Sir R.G. Bhandarkar*, 4 vols (Bhandarkar Oriental Research Institute, Puna, 1928–33), II: 624–38.

68. Ibid., p. 637.

69. R.G. Bhandarkar, 'Presidential Address at the Bombay Provincial Social Conference', 1902 (Sholapur). Paranjape and Utgikar (eds), *Collected Works of Sir R.G. Bhandarkar*, vol. II, pp. 518–26.

70. R.G. Bhandarkar, 'The Critical, Comparative, and Historical Method of Inquiry', Paranjape and Utgikar (eds), *Collected Works of Sir R.G. Bhandarkar*, vol. II p. 391.

71. R.G. Bhandarkar, 'Convocation Address, Bombay University', 1894, in Paranjape and Utgikar (eds), *Collected Works of Sir R.G. Bhandarkar*, vol. I, pp. 447–8.

72. Ibid., p. 450.

73. R.G Bhandarkar, 'The Ends and Aims of College Education', Address at Deccan College, Poone, 1893, Paranjape and Utgikar (eds), *Collected Works of Sir R.G. Bhandarkar*, pp. 465–6.

74. Ibid.

75. R.G. Bhandarkar, 'The Critical, Comparative, and Historical Method of Inquiry', lecture delivered in March 1888, in Paranjape and Utgikar (eds), *Collected Works of Sir R.G. Bhandarkar*, vol. I, p. 392; the entire essay is valuable as a statement of the agenda of the author's lifework.

76. R.G. Bhandarkar, 'Inaugural Address at Bhandarkar Oriental Research Institute', 15 December 1918, in Paranjape and Utgikar (eds), *Collected Works of Sir R.G. Bhandarkar* , vol. I, pp. 416–21.

77. R.G. Bhandarkar 'Presidential Address at the Bombay Provincial Social Conference, 1902', Paranjape and Utgikar (eds), *Collected Works of Sir R.G. Bhandarkar*, vol. II , pp. 518–23.

78. 'Rejoinder to Mr Ranade', in Paranjape and Utgikar (eds), *Collected Works of Sir R.G. Bhandarkar*, vol. II, p. 453.

79. R.G Bhandarkar, 'Speech in Imperial Legislative Council, Indian Universities Bill, 1904,' *Debates in Imperial Legislative Council*, pp. 176, 332, 334–5, cited in Bhattacharya *et.al.* (eds), *Educating the Nation: Documents on the Discourse of National Education in India 1880–1920* (Kanishka, Jawaharlal Nehru University, Delhi, 2003), pp. 278–9 (emphasis mine).

CHAPTER 2

Mahatma Gandhi and the Nationalist Discourse of Civilization

In considering Mahatma Gandhi's position in the discourse of civilization we shall take *Hind Swaraj* as the central text. This work was written in 1909 while Gandhi was on a ship, returning from England. He wrote it first in his own mother tongue. Next year, in 1910, he translated the Gujarati version into English and published it from Johannesburg. It is a tract which seems to come straight from the heart; it is not dressed up in the language of nationalist politicians of that age. All the editions of this tract were published in South Africa till 1919; by that time *Hind Swaraj* had acquired such a reputation that the first Indian edition published in 1919, was reprinted and sold out six times in the next five years. It was a sort of bestseller.

In a preface written by Gandhi on board the ship sailing from England, he said: 'These views are mine and yet not mine. They are mine because I hope to act according to them. They are almost a part of my being. But yet they are not mine because I lay no claim to originality....These views are held by many Indians not touched by what is known as civilization....'[1] Thus *Hind Swaraj* was an unusual political tract that from the very beginning focuses on civilizational issues; political pronouncements are derived from that. To Gandhi the crux of the matter was the clash between cultures or you might say in a broader sense clash between different paradigms of human existence inherent in two different civilizations, modern European civilization and ancient Indian civilization.

Further, Gandhi makes it amply clear that the political battle for independence was secondary compared to the clash of cultures in the encounter between India and Europe. 'It is my deliberate opinion that India is being ground down not under the English heel, but under that of modern civilization.'[2] Again he writes: 'It is not necessary for us to have as our goal the expulsion of the English....We can accommodate them. Only there is no room for their civilization.'[3] Or again he surmises that most Indian politicians want 'English rule without Englishman', that is, they would like to 'make India English'. 'This is not the *Swaraj* that I want.'[4] In 1910, Gandhi wrote in his journal *Indian Opinion* (1910): 'We saw in *Hind Swaraj* that it is not so much from *British Rule* that we have to save ourselves, as from Western civilization.'[5]

In these and similar statements Gandhi clearly subordinates the political programme to the cultural agenda. It is an odd sort of political tract that subordinates the political to the cultural, but that is what *Hind Swaraj* is about. In fact Gandhi underlined this fact in his new preface to the South Africa edition in 1910: the issue, he said, was not the stability or overthrow of the British Empire, the issue was the integrity of Indian civilization or culture. 'I must frankly confess that I am not so much concerned about the stability of the Empire as I am about that of the ancient civilization of India which in my opinion is the best the world has ever seen.'[6]

These are the reasons why in addressing the question of Gandhi's approach to the issue of civilization, we choose the book *Hind Swaraj* as our basic text. That apart, it is well known that *Hind Swaraj* as a text enjoys a centrality in Gandhi's corpus of works. Let us recall that Gandhi says in the last lines of the book that 'my life henceforth is dedicated to the attainment of the ideals' stated in *Hind Swaraj*. And that Gandhi says in the first few lines of the book: these views 'are almost a part of my being.'[7]

Before we go any further let us pay attention to three characteristics of this text. First, Gandhi speaks throughout this book of the *Indian* Civilization not of the *Hindu* Civilization. Although the content of many of the concepts and values he expounds form a part of Hindu civilization, Gandhi never substituted the category of 'Indian civilization' with 'Hindu culture or civilization'. 'Should we not remember that many Hindu and Mohammedans own the same ancestors and the same blood runs through their veins? Is the God of the Mohammedan different from the God of the Hindu? Religions are different roads converging to the same point.'[8] Culture may have its roots in religious belief-systems but its fruits are values which are common to humanity as a whole. Gandhi recognizes one distinct element in the Islamic belief system: 'Islam's distinct contribution to India's culture', he believed, was an 'unadulterated belief in the oneness of God and practical application of the truth of the brotherhood of man for those nominally within its field.' [9]

An important element in the nationalist discourse of civilization was the idea of 'syncretism'. *Hind Swaraj* contains one of the earliest formulations of this notion. Gandhi writes that India has 'the faculty of assimilation'. Between Shaivites and Vaishnavas there had been in the past deadly conflicts; 'vedic religion is different from Jainism'; but nevertheless they all belong to the same nation.[10] These are, of course, views which Gandhi expressed times without number throughout his life. But there are interesting amendments in the *Hind Swaraj* text. In chapter X in the original version, published in 1909, it was said: 'If the Hindus believe that India should be peopled only by Hindus, they are living in dreamland. The Mohamedans also live in dreamland if they believe that there should be only Muslims in India.' In 1939 the revised version of *Hind Swaraj* from Nava Jivan Press omitted the second sentence. This omission might have been merely to avoid repetition or redundancy. Or it might have been a concession to the political situation prevailing in 1939. What comes out loud and clear in *Hind Swaraj* is that Gandhi talks of *Indian* civilization as a category comprehending different streams of culture regardless of religious denomination. In 1939 Gandhi reports in *Harijan* a conversation with a Muslim interlocutor.[11] Gandhi was asked: Do you cherish Muslim culture 'as you would cherish your own Hindu culture?' Gandhi's reply was that he did not 'aim at any fusion' of the two religions; but 'I believe Islam and other great religions to be as true as my own. India is richer for the cultures that Islam and Christianity brought with them.'[12]

Since Gandhi conceptualizes culture as a set of norms or a way of life, he contended that culture is not to be identified with material objects like books and art treasures and monuments. In an interview with Reverend Ting-fang Lew, a Christian missionary from China, in December 1938 he said culture does not reside in buildings and books and so on, 'A nation's culture resides in the heart and soul of its people'—and thus Japanese destruction of Chinese libraries and monuments would be of no consequence.[13] Gandhi might have had in mind the occasional incidents of destruction of temples and mosques in India.

The second interesting characteristic of the text *Hind Swaraj* is that it is written in the form of a dialogue, a series of questions and answers, arguments and counter-arguments. This is the only work of its kind written by Gandhi. Why did he choose this form? Many traditional texts in India are in this form of a dialogue. The *Gita* is a prominent instance. Gandhi says in his autobiography that he read the *Gita* when he was in his teens as he was attracted to its representation of the 'duel in the minds of men'. Perhaps Gandhi chose this form in *Hind Swaraj* because of the influence of the *Gita* on his mind. There was perhaps also a greater purpose: he wanted to represent in this form the dialogue between the West and East,

which is the theme of the book. That, indeed, may be the answer to
the question why the book is written in the form of a dialogue by
Gandhi. It is, of course, also possible that Gandhi adopted this form
'to make it easy reading.'[14] But Gandhi never used the same form
in writing any other book to make it easy to read. In this instance
he might as well have chosen the dialogue form for the reasons we
have suggested.

The third characteristic of *Hind Swaraj* is a gross simplification
of a complex European culture. The same essentialization which
Edward Said criticized[15] in the Western discourse on the orient,
known as *Orientalism*, is also seen in Gandhi's essentialism vis-à-
vis the West. Gandhi talks of the Western civilization as if it was
homogeneous when it was obviously not. In fact, it contained great
diversity. Gandhi talks of the West as the repository of certain values
like materialism, consumerism, selfish self indulgence, unbridled
technological development detrimental to Nature and man, and
many others. And yet Gandhi was not unfamiliar with the West—he
had access to West European culture, or at least English culture; he
had spent a good deal of time in England; and in fact he also quotes
Western authors who were critical of some aspects of modern
Western civilization—such as John Ruskin, Count Tolstoy, Schlegel,
Edward Carpenter, Thoreau and others who exemplify a contrary
tradition within Western culture.

So, why this essentialist and simplistic representation of the West
in Gandhi? A plausible answer can be that Gandhi was writing
for the purpose of propaganda—that he was stringing together
in *Hind Swaraj* a series of charges against England or the West
in order to undermine its moral authority. Gandhi was doing this
notwithstanding his knowledge that this essentialism was untrue to
reality. But is that a satisfactory answer? Is it plausible that Gandhi
was stringing together a set of untruths about the West to glorify the
East, its 'other'? So then, why this essentialism, this counterfactual
tirade against the Western civilization? For the present we will not
try to answer the question, we will come back to it later.

Hind Swaraj anticipated a notion that the nationalist discourse on civilization elaborated later. This was the notion that India possessed civilizational unity long before British rule brought about an administrative unity. Gandhi is aware that nationhood in India was in the process of developing but he underlined what he considered the more important unity India had as a civilization.

In the beginning of *Hind Swaraj* he postulates that 'Nations are not formed in a day, the formation requires years....As time passes the Nation is being forged.'[16] And he thought that in the process of nation formation the Swadeshi movement in Bengal against Partition had played a crucial role. 'The demand for the abrogation of the Partition is tantamount to a demand for Home Rule. Leaders in Bengal know this. British officials realize it....The shock the British power received through the Partition [agitation] has never been equalled by any other act....The spirit generated in Bengal has spread in the north to the Punjab and in the south to Cape Comorin.'[17] While he observed that India was a nation in making, Gandhi maintained that the essence of nationhood had reposed in the Indian way of life even before British rule began. 'Our thought inspired us. Our mode of life was the same.'[18] He pointed to the unifying factors despite cultural differences within: 'They learned one another's languages, and there was no aloofness between them.' The location of pilgrimage centres in various places from Rameshwaram in the extreme south to Hardwar in the north, Gandhi surmised, was intended to promote a feeling of unity. The 'far-seeing ancestors of ours' must have deliberately 'established holy places in various parts of India, and fired people with an idea of nationality....' It was 'the English who taught us that we were not one nation before [British rule] and that it will require centuries before we become one nation....Only you and I and others who consider ourselves civilized and superior persons imagine that we are many nations.'[19] At the end of the book in a final conversation between the author and his interlocutor, the 'Reader', the latter asks 'what will you say to the nation?' And the author asks in turn a crucial question, 'who is the nation?' Gandhi's answer is that only those 'who conscientiously believe that Indian civilization is the best' can represent the nation and say to the British rulers, 'We hold the civilization that you support to be the reverse of civilization.'[20]

To sum up, Gandhi suggests that although prior to British rule there were elements in Indian civilization which contained seeds of national unity, under British rule those seeds were in the custody of only those untouched by Western or modern civilization. In political resistance to British rule, for example, in Bengal's anti-partition agitation, nationhood was being forged, but the ultimate test of integration with the nation was identification with Indian civilization. This stance is consistent with the general trend of argument in this work prioritizing the concept of civilization over that of nationhood. As we shall see later, Rabindranath Tagore went much farther in the same direction. Tagore's disillusionment with the limits of nationalism led him to cling more firmly to the concept of India's civilizational personality and unity. In both Tagore and Gandhi's writings civilizational unity was a surrogate for national unity.

While the concept of civilization was at the core of *Hind Swaraj*, there was another idea which Gandhians in later times emphasized much more and this was the creed of non-violence. A few days before Gandhi began to write that work, we find him writing to his political guru, G.K. Gokhale: among the Indians he met in London 'most consider that violence is the only method' in the struggle for *swaraj*.[21] Later, in a new edition of *Hind Swaraj* in 1921, Gandhi wrote in a Preface that in 1908 he had 'come in contact with every known Indian anarchist in London' and he formed the impression that it was necessary to provide an 'answer to the Indian school of violence.'[22] Hence, *Hind Swaraj* contained several homilies about the unwisdom of taking to a path of violence. However, this political message was not as important in that text as the more general argument about civilizations; in 1921 and thereafter the message of non-violence in that text was highlighted for obvious political reasons.

The above-mentioned political message in *Hind Swaraj* was, however, secondary in importance in Gandhi's scheme of things. As we have noted earlier, in this text the political issues are consistently subordinated to the civilizational issues. Gandhi begins the book with the question 'What is true civilization?'—which is the title of a chapter. Gandhi's answer to the question is complex. He says that material artifacts do not exhaustively define civilization. For there are people who possess these material artifacts but are not considered civilized or cultured. Thus a cultured English gentleman looks down upon the new rich who may have more material possessions than the aristocrat or the gentleman. Gandhi goes on to say that being cultured or civilized is, therefore, a question of the cultivation of the mind. Thus the Greeks were more civilized than the Romans who conquered them. Having established this distinction between advancement in the materialist sense and advancement in the cultivation of the mind, Gandhi goes on to develop a rather simplistic argument. This argument is that Europe in the beginning of the twentieth century represented materialism in its worst manifestations or forms.

The characteristic of 'materialistic civilization' which Gandhi found reprehensible in Europe were many. But analytically speaking one may divide them into four sets or groups. In Gandhi's thought there appear to be basically four binary oppositions which lie at the foundation of his exposition. First, the opposition between competition and cooperation; second, the divide between machine and nature; third, the opposition between self-denial and consumerism and self-indulgence; and fourth, the tension between statism and communitarianism in the realm of the polity.

To proceed analytically we shall now look at each of these binary opposites:

(A) In rejecting competition in favour of cooperation, Gandhi evidently rejects the fundamental engine of capitalist society. In the manner of Tolstoy and Ruskin, Gandhi suggests cooperative activities as an alternative to competition which pushes capitalism forward. Gandhi was familiar with Adam Smith's classic, *Wealth of Nations*, a work he cited more than once in his writings. Gandhi points out that among the economic principles and laws, which are supposed to be universal and absolute, is the principle of competition. He looked upon this principle as the opposite of the Indian scheme of things: 'We have had no system of life-corroding competition.'[23] Gandhi held up the spirit of non-competitive cooperation as the superior principle. Competition which was the central idea of classical economic thinking since the rise of capitalism Gandhi rejects. This was tantamount to rejecting the concept of the *homo economicus*, a rejection of the market principle for it was competition in the market which would decide values and prices of products and services. Gandhi's idea of cooperation, as opposed to competition, brings to mind a similar stance of the Utopian socialists and syndicalists. In *Hind Swaraj* Gandhi explicitly acknowledged his indebtedness to at least two socialists—John Ruskin and Edward Carpenter.[24] The latter in fact was influenced deeply by Frederick Engels and Lewis Morgan. Needless to say, Gandhi does not refer to Engels or Marx. But a distant echo of the theory of private property in relation to the state, and Ruskin's views on the bourgeois political economy founded upon self-interest, are evident in Gandhi's *Hind Swaraj*.

(B) The second anti-thesis in *Hind Swaraj* is that between Nature and machinery. To a practical mind like Gandhi's the aspect of modern science that was most relevant was technology or machinery. This part of Gandhian thought has recently attracted a lot of attention because of the environmentalists' concern about ecological damages caused by uncontrolled technology. The same theme found a different, more artistic and aesthetic expression, in nineteenth century England in the writings of William Blake on the 'dark satanic mills', the poetry of the Romantics, and the paintings of the pre-Raphaelites in England. In Gandhi the reaction to industrial technology is not scientific as in the modern environmentalist movement, nor aesthetic as was the case with the European Romantics. It is primarily a

social and ethical reaction in Gandhi. To him the machinery of
modern industrial civilization meant the destruction of a society's
equilibrium with Nature; hence his insistence on the evils of city
life and the virtues of rural life. City life dominated and served
by machinery was contrasted by Gandhi with village life where
man directly interacted with Nature unmediated by machines.
Of course man uses tools and machines in farming or in forestry
or in fishing. But Gandhi's point was that such machines are
controlled by the man at work whereas the bigger and more
complex machines in industry are not controlled by the man
who works but by others. This looks like the notion of alienation
under industrial capitalism but actually it is different. Gandhi's
approach contains a heavy emphasis on the moral aspects of life
in the industrial city and the moral superiority of the rural life
pattern—and Marx, as we know, had nothing but contempt for
'rural idiocy', the low level of consciousness of the peasantry.
Like a true successor to the Enlightenment tradition Marx was
all for technological advancement in the man–Nature dialectics;
Gandhi, on the other hand, speaks like the Nature worshippers
of early India and turns his back on the machine age.

There were also two other factors in the anti-mechanization
stance in Gandhi. He blamed machinery for the decline of
the handicraft industry, Khadi or handspun and handwoven
textile industry in the British period. The increase in import of
Manchester cotton textiles was described by Gandhi to show
how India's own pre-factory textile industry was destroyed, and
how India was de-industrialized. 'When I read Mr R.C. Dutt's
Economic History of India, I wept....It is machinery which has
impoverished India.'[25] Second, while that had happened in the past,
in the future Gandhi strongly de-recommended mechanization
because it would reduce employment, by replacing human beings
with machines in an economy which had surplus manpower.
Thus his economic sense merged with a moral fervour to push
Gandhi towards an anti-mechanization stance. Shortly before he
wrote *Hind Swaraj*, the Swadeshi movement had developed in

Bengal from 1905 and Gandhi writes; 'I was delighted when I read about the bravery of Bengal' but that boycott 'encouraged the mill industry of Bombay. If Bengal had proclaimed a boycott of all machine-made goods, it would have been much better.'[26]

(C) The third antithesis posited in Gandhi's philosophy is between consumerism and avoidance of self-indulgence. He wrote a good deal on the supposed Indian tradition here which is open to question. For example, 'The mind is a restless bird, the more it gets the more it wants, and still remains unsatisfied. The more we indulge our passions, the more unbridled they become. Our ancestors [the Hindu sages] therefore set a limit to our indulgence. They dissuaded us from luxuries and pleasures ...' [27]

The problem with this is not only that it glorifies technological stagnation. It also fails to answer the question: what is self-indulgence? One man's self-indulgence may be another man's necessity. Where does one draw a line? But Gandhi is not interested in the question, obvious as it is. Indeed he dexterously turns his critique of excessive consumption into a political agenda for India. He says that if Indians cease to consume the British goods imported to India it will hurt the British where it hurts them most, their pocket. 'Napoleon is said to have described the English as a nation of shopkeepers. They hold whatever dominion they have for the sake of their commerce....The English wish to convert the whole world into a vast market for their goods.'[28] Having thus characterized the continuous expanded reproduction in world capitalism—without using those concepts—Gandhi says that to reduce consumption is a means of counteracting and diminishing British imperialism. From this later developed his battle-cry: 'Boycott British Goods'!

(D) Fourth, there is an anti-thesis postulated by Gandhi between statism and communitarianism. He suggests that statism is integral to European culture while the Indian ideal was the opposite. Gandhi looks at the British historical experience and he says that he is sceptical of the state, he is sceptical of the parliamentary system depending on party system, he is sceptical of the media which forms public opinion, he is sceptical of the judicial system where lawyers defend a client for money and so on. Thus emerges a philosophy of anarchism or anti-statism in Gandhi. He wanted a state of enlightened anarchy in which each person would become his own ruler. In his ideal state there would be no political institutions and therefore no political power. Instead there will be the community of citizens; a collection of self-regulating communities will form the polity.

These are the four antithesis which Gandhi presents: he is all for cooperation and opposed to competition in the market, he is against the machine especially in his conflict with Nehru, he is for self-denial opposed to consumerism, and he is for anarchic communitarianism as opposed to the State as we know it in the West in the twentieth century.

Some of his statements in *Hind Swaraj* of 1909, Gandhi modified later. For example he wrote in 1921: 'I am not aiming at destroying railways and hospitals though I would certainly welcome their natural destruction....they are a necessary evil....Nor am I aiming at a permanent destruction of law courts....Still less I am trying to destroy all machinery and mills.'[29] However, Gandhi maintained his original position in *Hind Swaraj*—condemnation of Western and modern civilization. 'I have ventured utterly to condemn modern civilization because I hold that the spirit of it is evil. It is possible to show that some of its incidents are goods, but I have examined the tendency in the scale of ethics.' Gandhi wrote thus to a friend and associate, Wybergh soon after publishing *Hind Swaraj*.[30] In that sweeping condemnation it is obvious that Gandhi over-simplifies things. He simplifies the vast and various occidental civilization, he ignores contrary intellectual and philosophical trends within that civilization, he highlights only those aspects of the modern European civilization which he wished the world would reject. This is what we have called an essentialist representation of the West.

Why did Gandhi choose to do this, though he knew that things were not as simple as that? I suggest that Gandhi is using the West as a metaphor. This is the source of Gandhi's essentialism, despite his knowledge of ambiguities and complexities of history and of cultures. This is one possible way to read *Hind Swaraj*, without attributing to Gandhi crass ignorance or plain dishonesty.

Gandhi's object, I suggest, was to represent Europe as the essence of one aspect of the human mind, that which creates machines to subordinate Nature, that which drives man as *homo economicus* to endless consumption, that which acquires power for its own sake in the spheres of economy and politics and knowledge. Against this representation of Europe, Gandhi posited another essentialist representation of the East and endowed that with opposite values. It was in a way the replication of the rhetorical strategy of the *Gita,* in that Gandhi invites us to look at the duality in the minds of men. Therefore, I suggest that in reading Gandhi's *Hind Swaraj* we have to read the West as a metaphor, standing for one aspect of the human mind. When Gandhi makes statements in the metaphorical mode it will be a mistake to read them literally as descriptive statements regarding historical reality.

This argument, the distinction between 'the West-as-a-metaphor' and 'the West as a historical category' may not be acceptable to those who might see in it an artifice to 'rationalize' the message in *Hind Swaraj*. But the distinction appears to be sustainable if one examines the trend in Gandhi's pronouncements on the question from 1909 till his death. At times Gandhi uses the West as a metaphor for a type of civilization he condemned, and at other times he speaks in another mode about the West as a historical reality and makes judgements of a different kind.

For example, Gandhi is speaking in the second mode in 1921: 'I am no hater of the West. I am thankful to the West for many things I have learnt from Western literature'—though India should eschew the 'worship of the material' in that civilization.[31] Again, in 1929: 'It is not my purpose even to imply that everything Western is bad. I have learnt a lot from the West.'[32] Or again in 1940: 'When I described modern civilization, symbolized in imperialism, as godless in *Hind Swaraj*, I know that I had nothing but goodwill towards those who represented it.'[33] Such statements were not universalist generalizations in condemnation of the West, they recognized particularities within that civilization as things worthy of regard. At the same time, Gandhi rarely made such statements without qualification.

First, that was a culture of the conquerors. Most telling was a childhood memory he recounts in 1940. He recalls that when he was a child his father had to attend as an official a *Durbar* on the occasion of the visit of the Governor.

> Our household was turned upside down when my father had to attend the Durbar during a Governor's visit. He never wore stockings or boots or what were then called 'whole boots'. His general foot-wear was soft leather slippers. It I was a painter, I could paint my father's disgust and torture on his face as he was putting his legs into his stockings and his feet into ill-
'tting and uncomfortable boots. He had to do this![34]

ndhi's point was the culture of the West was a part of the 'cultural
quest of India.'[35] The other illustration he provided was that
n aristocratic families discarded their traditional apparel in
· India: 'the Rajas and Maharajas looked like second editions
nsamas' [that is, waiters or chefs, generally native servants
nglish household]. And Gandhi goes on to describe how
e certain genuflections prescribed for Indians in a levee
In short, the so-called Western culture in British-ruled
ented a cultural hegemony and a 'cultural and spiritual
of Indians.[36]
· other qualification Gandhi repeatedly made was
cultural as a moral one.[37] Even before Gandhi left
November 1909 (the journey during which he
ʒj) his views were deeply influenced by Edward
ation: Its Causes and Cure. The substance of
ue of European civilization in *Hind Swaraj* is
his letter to his friend H. Polak on 14 October
ɔn of the idea that a morally unacceptable

materialistic civilization in Europe should be resisted was, as we have seen, at the core of *Hind Swaraj*. Gandhi was asked time and again throughout his life whether he stood by the position he had taken in that book vis-à-vis the West. Five years after its first publication in the Preface to the second Gujarati edition in 1914 Gandhi asserted that he remained 'an uncompromising enemy of the present day civilization of Europe'.[39] In 1921 the preface to an English edition reiterated: 'I withdraw nothing except one word of it, and that in deference to a lady friend.'[40] (The word 'prostitute' was dropped in a description of the Parliament in England.) In 1931 when a reporter of the *Chicago Tribune* asked him if he had revised his opinion since he wrote *Hind Swaraj*' Gandhi replied that his 'ideas about the evils of Western civilization still stand.'[41] In 1938 Gandhi writes that after a 'stormy thirty years' his views stated in *Hind Swaraj* remained the same; 'I have seen nothing to make me alter the views expounded in it'.[42] In 1945 he writes to Jawaharlal Nehru on similar lines. Nehru wrote hoping that Gandhi's ideas had probably changed since 1909. 'In your writings and speeches since then I have found much that seemed to me an advance on that old position and an appreciation of modern trends.'[43] But Gandhi stood his ground and stated with reference to *Hind Swaraj*: 'My experience has confirmed the truth of what I wrote in 1909. If I am the only one left who believed in it, I would not be sorry.'[44]

Setting aside for the moment Gandhi's own comments cited ealier, does his writing indeed indicate that he revised the stance he took in 1909 regarding civilization in the West and in India? It is possible that since he entered the thick of Indian politics in 1919 he ceased to emphasize the absolute and uncompromising ideals held up in *Hind Swaraj*. In fact his mentor G.K. Gokhale supposedly predicted this in 1912. Mahadev Desai writes that when Gokhale saw the English translation of the book 'he prophesied that Gandhiji himself would destroy the book after spending a year in India.'[45] Gandhi did not disown the book, but a slight change of inflection might have occurred from 1919 when he was at the head of a political movement involving people of various persuasions. Moreover, the debates Gandhi entered into in response to Rabindranath Tagore's critique of his ideas about rural industry as a substitute for factory system of production, the viability of Khadi, boycott as a political weapon, and so on, widened into more generic issues.[46] Should India reject Western culture entirely and eradicate it root and branch in India or should that eradication be discriminating? Should India aim at a return to her ancient past and take to the strait and narrow path shown by the sages? How should India address those features of her society and culture which were supported by tradition but evidently negated rationality and impeded her progress? The result of this debate was that while Tagore became more aware of the art of practical politics, Gandhi was probably more alert to the limits of the idea of a civilization dependent upon sages and ancestors. Gandhi wrote in 1909: 'I believe that the civilization India has evolved is not to be beaten in the world. Nothing can equal the seeds sown by our ancestors…India has nothing to learn from anybody else and this is as it should be.'[47] Compare that to the openness of his response to Tagore in 1921: 'I will not want my house to be walled in all sides and windows to be stuffed. I want the culture of all the lands to be blown about my house as freely as possible. But I refuse to be blown off my feet by any.'[48] It was a fine change of inflexion.

About this time, while the debate between Gandhi and Tagore was going on in journals, Gandhi made several statements also suggesting a change in his attitude. For instance in the article 'Living on the Past' in 1920 he said that Indians cannot afford to live on their past glory and are Indians indeed worthy of their heritage?[49] Next week in another essay Gandhi writes: just as 'a son cannot live on his father's reputation for long' India cannot live on past glories.[50] Gandhi sometimes returns to the theme and refines the notions formulated in *Hind Swaraj*. 'I would ask you', he said to Gandhi Seva Sangha members in 1939, 'to read *Hind Swaraj* with my eyes….You cannot build non-violence on a factory civilization…. Rural economy as I have conceived it eschews exploitation altogether and exploitation is the essence of violence.'[51] Again in his journal *Harijan* in 1939: 'I am working for a civilization in which possession of a car will be considered no merit,' but at the same time 'being a highly practical man I do not avoid railway traveling or motoring for the mere sake of looking foolishly consistent.'[52] He went on to say about *Hind Swaraj*: 'it is not an attempt to get back to the so-called ignorant, dark ages. But it is an attempt to see beauty in voluntary simplicity, poverty, and slowness. I have pictured that as my ideal. I shall never reach it myself and hence cannot expect the nation to do so.'[53]

When Gandhi thus talks of 'factory civilization' as a thing built on violence since it involves exploitation, or when he talks of 'the beauty in voluntary simplicity', he is making highly nuanced statements compared to what he said earlier, for instance: 'Modern civilization is chiefly materialistic, ours is chiefly spiritual.'[54] The latter type of statement was open to obtuse reading, liable to take the metaphorical idiom he used in a literal sense. This is why earlier in this chapter we have made a distinction between the metaphorical and the historical categories in Gandhi's writings on civilization.

We may conclude with a touching letter Gandhi wrote to Nehru towards the end of his life. He writes on 5 October 1945 to explicate what his vision stood for, both in 1909 and in 1945.

My ideal village still exists only in my imagination. After all every human being lives in the world of his own imagination. In this village of my dreams the villager will not be dull—he will be all awareness. He will not live like an animal in filth and darkness. Men and women will live in freedom, prepared to face the whole world...Nobody will be allowed to be idle or to wallow in luxury. Everyone will have to do body labour....[55]

And Gandhi also explained his stress on 'simplicity'. He seems to say that complexity and largeness of scale in systems, technology, governance is detrimental to the individual's freedoms. 'The sum and substance of what I want to say is that the individual person should have control over the things that are necessary for the substance of life. If he cannot have such control the individual cannot survive. Ultimately the world is made up only of individuals.' What is touching about this letter is the anxiety of an old man to make himself understood, a desperation in conceding that perhaps his ideals existed only in his imagined world, and also a willingness to embrace the solitude to which he is exiled when no one else shared his vision. When he calls that vision his 'dreams' he recognizes its distance from historical reality, and yet he thus reaffirms the ideas inscribed in that vision. 'I work for a civilization', he once wrote—a civilization that would be different from the Western or modern civilization. By the end of his life he came to recognize his loneliness in the pursuit of the civilization he had imagined. 'If I were the only one left in the world who believed in it, I would not be sorry.'[56]

Today, in the light of the history of our own times, many aspects of Gandhi's thoughts acquire a new meanings. His rejection of competition in the market, the basis of capitalist society, demands our attention today when the market culture has overwhelmed and virtually obliterated the social-welfare philosophy and agenda of action in most countries. His critique of unbridled elaboration of industrial technology calls for our attention at a time when technology threatens the ecological balance in Nature and global environment. His opposition to consumerism as an end in itself appeals to many people in high consumption cultures—people who may be a minority, but a significant minority. His community-based approach pointing to decentralized participatory self-government and initiative from the civil society outside of the State has raised echoes in the minds of those who organize non-government communitarian initiatives with a social purpose. And finally, his contraposition of different paradigms of civilization seems more urgently relevant when there is taking place in our times the homogenization of the culture of the entire world on the North American pattern.

NOTES

1. *Hind Swaraj* (*HS* hereafter), *Collected Works of Mahatma Gandhi* (*CWMG* hereafter) (Publications Division, New Delhi, 1999), vol. 10, p. 7.
2. Ibid., p. 24.
3. Ibid., p. 39.
4. Ibid., p. 15.

5. *Indian Opinion*, 22 October 1910, *CWMG*, vol. 10, p. 134.

6. M.K. Gandhi, 'The Publication of Indian Home Rule', *Indian Opinion*, Johannesburg, 20 March 1910; *CWMG*, vol. 10, pp. 188–90.

7. *HS*, *CWMG*, vol. 10, pp. 7, 64.

8. Ibid., p. 29.

9. Gandhi in interview with John Mott, *Young India*, vol. 21, no. 3, 1929; *CWMG*, vol. 40, p. 58.

10. *HS*, *CWMG*, vol. 10, p. 28.

11. *Harijan*, 28 January 1939.

12. *CWMG*, vol. 78, p. 323.

13. *CWMG*, vol. 78, p. 263.

14. *HS*, *CWMG*, vol. 10, p. 7.

15. Edward Said, *Orientalism* (Pantheon Books, London, 1978).

16. *CWMG*, vol. 10, p. 12.

17. Ibid., pp. 12–3.

18. Ibid., p. 27.

19. Ibid., p. 27.

20. Ibid., p. 61.

21. Gandhi to G.K. Gokhale, 11 November 1909, *CWMG*, vol. 9, pp. 531–2.

22. *Young India*, January 1921.

23. *HS*, *CWMG*, vol. 10, p. 37.

24. Ibid., pp. 65–8.

25. Ibid., p. 57.

26. Ibid., p. 58.

27. Ibid., p. 36.

28. Ibid., p. 23.

29. Gandhi, 'A Word of Explanation', *HS*, edition of 1921, reprinted in *Young India*, January 1921.

30. Gandhi to W.J. Wyberg, 10 May 1910, *CWMG*, vol. 10, p. 247.

31. Speech in Calcutta, 23 January 1921, *CWMG*, vol. 19, pp. 266–7.

32. *Young India*, 28 April 1929; *CWMG*, vol. 40, p. 300.

33. *Harijan*, 3 February 1940, *CWMG*, vol. 71, pp. 150–3.

34. Ibid., p. 152.

35. Ibid.

36. Ibid.

37. M.K. Gandhi (in London) to H.S.L. Polak, 9 September 1909, *CWMG*, vol. 9, p. 396.

38. M.K. Gandhi to H. Polak, 14 October 1909, *CWMG*, vol. 9, pp. 477–82.

39. Preface to second Gujarati edition of *Hind Swaraj* reprinted in *Indian Opinion*, 29 April 1914, *CWMG*, vol. 12, pp. 411–12.

40. M.K. Gandhi, 'A Word of Explanation', in the English edition of *Hind Swaraj*, 1921, reprinted in *Young India*, January, 1921.

41. *CWMG*, vol. 45, pp. 332–3.

42. M.K. Gandhi, 14 July 1938, *Aryan Path*, September 1938.

43. Nehru to Gandhi, *Selected Works of Jawaharlal Nehru*, vol. 14, p. 554, 9 October 1945.

44. Gandhi to Nehru, 5 October 1945, *CWMG*, vol. 81, p. 319.

45. Mahadev Desai, 8 February 1938, in *Aryan Path: Special Hind Swaraj* Nivas, September 1938, reprinted in M.K. Gandhi, *Hind Swaraj* (Navjivan Publishing House, Ahmedabad, 1938, reprint of 2006, p. 14).

46. Sabyasachi Bhattacharya (ed.), 'Editor's Introduction', *The Mahatma and the Poet: Letters and debates between Gandhi and Tagore, 1915–1941* (National Book Trust, Delhi, 2005, 3rd reprint), pp. 1–37.

47. *HS, CWMG*, vol. 10, pp. 36–7.

48. Gandhi, 'The Great Sentinel', *Young India*, June 1921.

49. Gandhi 'Living on the Past', *Navjivan*, 20 June 1920, *CWMG*, vol. 17, p. 515.

50. *Navjivan*, 27 June 1920; *CWMG*, vol. 17, p. 515.

51. Gandhi's address to Sevagram, Wardha, 25 October 1939, *CWMG*, vol. 70, p. 296.

52. Gandhi in reply to a correspondent, *Harijan*, 14 October 1939, *CWMG*, vol. 70, p. 242.

53. Ibid., p. 242.

54. Gandhi's address to Gurukul Ashram, 26 March 1916, *CWMG*, vol. 13, p. 261.

55. Gandhi to Nehru, 5 October 1945, *CWMG*, vol. 81, p. 319.

56. Ibid., p. 320.

CHAPTER 3

The Concept of Civilization

Rabindranath Tagore's Evolving Perspective

The idea of civilization plays a crucial role in Tagore's corpus of writings, especially in his essays on history, and society and politics in India. A few of these writings were written in English, and some of them are known chiefly through translation and long extracts in Nehru's *The Discovery of India*.[1] But a good number of the essays on this theme were written in the Bengali and they are scattered in twenty-six volumes of his collected works. It is necessary to consider for our study his writings in Bengali as well, because the writings in both languages are integrally connected and should be viewed as a whole. Tagore's approach to the issue of civilization in history evolved over a long period, roughly from 1870s to his last published work, *The Crisis of Civilization.*[2] Broadly one can distinguish four different phases in this evolution. In the first, 1877–1902 Tagore develops a sense of history from the nationalist point of view. This view, in the second phase from 1902–17, matures in the Swadeshi agitation days to a distinctively original perspective about Indian civilization. In 1902 a seminal essay on Indian history suggested the concept of 'a syncretic civilization.' In the third phase, from 1917–21 or thereabouts Tagore develops a critique of Europe's aggrandizing nationalism. He pereceived World War I as part of the global impact of that aggrandizing ideology. His identification with the spirit of nationalism, leading to his relinquishment of knighthood after Jallianwalla Bagh, produced a series of scathing essays on Western civilization in the context of the imperialism it had spawned and nurtured. In the last phase, 1921–41, Tagore's view of history was influenced by the perception that fault lines of community and caste threatened the notion of syncretic civilization he had nurtured for long years; further, the events of the World War II led to his disillusionment with that European Enlightenment which had at one time enriched India's Renaissance. For Tagore this last phase was one of painful re-interrogation of his earlier notions in a new light.

In the first phase one notices the development of Tagore's interest in Indian history but there is no engagement with the civilizational discourse. In 1877, when Tagore was seventeen years of age, he wrote his first essay on a historical theme, on the Rani of Jhansi. Next year young Tagore was sent off to England for a long stay. In 1885 Tagore again wrote a series of articles on Guru Nanak, Guru Gobind Singh, and the rise of Sikhism. An interest in heroic figures in the past was a part of the romantic trend in Bengal at that time. There was nothing remarkable in that except for the fact that Tagore showed a perspicacious judgement, at times against the grain of Bengali sentiment. For example, in writing about Lakshmi Bai, Tantia Tope, and Kunwar Singh he said: we feel inspired by their brave deeds as patriots, but 'we have no right to boast of their deeds'—an obvious allusion to the fact that the role of Bengal in the uprising of 1857 was absolutely marginal. The main idea which emerged from these early essays was that India needed histories written from the Indian point of view: 'what a misfortune it is for India that even the heroic life of the braves [of 1857] can be recovered only from the biased accounts of foreign historians.'[3] In another series of articles in 1898–9 Tagore underlined the same point in reviewing some Bengali works of history. This again was part of the cast of mind of the intellectuals in Bengal: Bankimchandra Chatterjee had written decades ago that the British write a history even if it is to record their safari to shoot birds, but where were Indian historians?[4] Tagore expresses similar sentiments but goes a little further. There is no doubt, he said, that India did not have the tradition of writing history as, for example, Greece and Rome. At the same time, he pointed out, there was a historical consciousness among the Rajputs, the Marathas since Shivaji (Tagore mentions the *bakhars*), and also among the Sikhs. These exceptions show that whenever there developed a political community with a sense of purpose, a historical consciousness also developed to bring together different isolates. Tagore explicitly makes a distinction here between religious and political communities and his examples make it clear that he means the political community as the site of such a process of development of historical consciousness. This is not too distant from the well-known viewpoint that the state alone has history. Be that as it may, Tagore's argument was that he saw a new national awakening in India in recent years and that inspired a new interest in the history of India. There had developed a 'hunger for history' which suggested that 'the Congress has not merely been memorializing the rulers year after year without any result—Congress has also...planted the seed of a new consciousness in our minds.'[5]

These thoughts led Tagore to elaborate his idea of history in a long essay entitled 'History of India' in 1902. In 1905 and again in 1908, that is, during the Swadeshi or anti-partition movement, the essay was revised and expanded. In this essay the agenda of nationally inspired history-writing is carried over from earlier years. The critique of British or colonial historiography of India is also developed. 'In a country favoured by fortune, people perceive in their histories, their own country, shaped by its past and in their childhood reading history introduces them to their own country. It is just the opposite in our country. Books of history hide from us our country.'[6] The textbooks of history were all about invasions and battles and the founding and dissolution of dynasties, not about the life of the people. 'In failing to look at India from our own point of view, we learn from our childhood to diminish India and thus to diminish our own selves.'[7] The question is, why are historical writings by the British flawed and inadequate? The answer Tagore was content with earlier was that these were written from the rulers' point of view, the commonly offered answer in those times. Tagore poses a new explanation, that there was a fundamental difference between the civilizations of Europe and India, and hence the apperception of India's history and civilization through European optics. European history is State-centred and 'its basis is aggrandizement; Indian civilization rests on syncretic unification'.[8]

***

The concept of a syncretic civilization in India became a fundamental element in the nationalist approach. One of the earliest expressions of this idea is to be found in Tagore's essay in 1902 on Indian history. There is a long passage which merits quotation.

We can see that the aim of Bharatvarsha has always been to establish unity amidst differences [or diversities], to bring to a convergence different paths, and to internalize within her soul the unity of the severalty, that is to say to comprehend the inner union between externally perceptible differences without eliminating the uniqueness of each element....Bharatvarsha has endeavoured to tie up diversities in a relationship. If there be genuine differences, it is possible to accommodate in its appropriate place such differences. You cannot legislate unity into existence. Elements which cannot assimilate need to be recognized and put in their appropriate separate places...Bharatvarsha knew the secret of this mode of unification ...Bharatvarsha limited the conflict between opposing and competing elements in society by keeping them separate and at the same time engaged in a common task that brought diverse elements together....[9]

Tagore reiterated this idea over and again, most notably in a long essay he wrote in 1912 entitled 'The Course of Indian History'.[10] Inferior to the essay of 1902, and somewhat speculative in nature, this essay attracted attention since Sir Jadunath Sarkar translated it into English for publication in *The Modern Review*. Here again Tagore argues: 'The endeavour of Indian has been to bring variousness into symmetrical unity.' For a long period stagnation had doubtless set in because the stabilizing system of India society, caste and shastric [scriptural] prescriptions, had itself become on obstacle to creativity and freedom of mind. But from the medieval Bhakti movement to the rise of Sikhism, there were contrary tendencies as well. Therefore Tagore surmised that the creative spirit of establishing unity amidst diversity inherent in Indian civilization would resuscitate India once again. Apropos to that, Tagore's critique of European civilization is notable. European civilization, being statist in character, used subordination as a means of protecting State power and thus to establish unity in the polity. 'The European way is to expel and to demolish all others for self-preservation—America, Australia, New Zealand, Cope Colony provide evidence of that.'[11]

This strand of thinking develops after the outbreak of World War I into a strident critique of the European notion of nationalism. The publication of the book *Nationalism* in 1917 marks a new phase in Tagore's thoughts on civilization. Since this work was available in English it has received much attention. These essays were written originally in English by Tagore as texts of lectures he delivered during his tour of Japan and USA from May 1916 to March 1917.[12] The historian E.P. Thompson has recently edited these essays and in his introductory essay he points to the obvious impact of the World War on Tagore's mind.[13] The War, Tagore argues, exposes the nature of European civilization: 'A political civilization has sprung up from the soil of Europe and is overrunning the whole world.... It is carnivorous and cannibalistic in its tendencies, it feeds upon

the resources of other peoples and tries to swallow their whole future.'[14] Or again: 'This civilization is the civilization of power, therefore it is exclusive, it is naturally unwilling to open its sources of power [science] to those whom it has selected for its purposes of exploitation....The truth is that the spirit of conflict and conquest is at the origin and in the centre of the Western nationalism.'[15] Western civilization gifted a State to India and that British Indian State is characterized by Tagore in these words:

Of all things in Western Civilization, those which this Western nation has given us in a most generous measure are law and order. While the small feeding bottle of our Education is nearly dry, and sanitation sucks its thumb in despair, military organisation, the magisterial offices, the police, the Criminal Investigation Department, the secret spy system, attain to an abnormal girth in their waists, occupying every inch of our country and we cannot but acknowledge this paradox that while the spirit of the West marches under its banners of freedom, the nation of this West forges its iron chains....[16]

Addressing his Japanese audience Tagore said: 'Not merely the subject races, but you who live under the delusion that you are free, are every day sacrificing your freedom and humanity to this fetish of nationalism....'[17] These ideas provoked a very adverse reaction in Japan as well as in the USA (where the lectures were published) and some Japanese intellectuals condemned these ideas as those typical of a defeated nation, India, and unworthy of attention in Japan.

And what of India? Tagore's basic notions about Indian civilization, were restated more firmly. The 'organized selfishness of Nationalism' was alien to Indian civilization. 'India has never had a real sense of nationalism. Even though from childhood I have been taught that the idolatry of Nation is almost better then reverence for God and humanity, I believe I have outgrown that teaching'; Tagore said that his conviction was that it was wrong to accept the view that 'a country is greater than an ideal of humanity.'[18] In India 'our ideals have been evolved through our own history' and India 'cannot borrow other people's history', that is, the history of European people who developed a national identity.[19] In contrast to the self-aggrandizement of European nationalism, often displayed in the extermination of other races (for example, in North America and Australia), India has 'tolerated differences of races from the first, and that spirit of toleration has acted all through her history.'[20]

Tagore also criticized the Indian nationalists' adulation of India's past. He cited examples: the caste system; 'the blind and lazy habit of relying upon the authority of traditions that are incongruous anachronisms in the present age'; 'the boundaries of immovable walls' separating communities. These are symptoms of 'social inadequacy' in the modern age but 'we have accepted as the creed of our nationalism that this social system has been perfected for all times to come by our ancestors' and hence a blind attempt to 'build a political miracle of freedom upon the quicksand of social slavery.' When there are such internal divisions can there be true political unity? Tagore surmised that the caste system was built in old times to forge 'a social unity within which all the different peoples could be held together, yet [each] fully enjoying the freedom of their own differences.' But its immutability is in modern times an anachronism, for 'mutability is the law of life.' For instance, in regulating trade interests caste might have served a purpose at one time, but since 'India laid all her emphasis upon the law of heredity' gradually the caste system 'reduced arts into crafts and genius into skill.' India must address these 'social inadequacies' before trying vainly to replicate the development of nationalism which occurred in some specific historical circumstances in the West. [21]

Since the work *Nationalism* is available in English it has attracted more attention. But one has to look at other essays, written about that time in Bengali; to get the full import of Tagore's pronouncements at this time. For instance, consider his essay of 1919 on 'The Study of Indian History'. He speaks with less confidence in 1919 than he did in 1902 about the success of India's assimilative civilization. Aware of the growing caste and communal divide, he writes: 'The difficult task of moulding diverse elements in society into unity without altogether erasing the specificities of each element has been attempted in India for a long time and the completion of the process remains unattained.'[22] He goes on to say that

some other countries like the USA were engaged in a similar endeavour since many races mingled there. But Tagore contended that
there were differences between the Indian and the North American
situation. First, in the USA those in the dominant ethnic group were
of European origin and between them 'there was no civilizational
schism.'[23] The new immigrants to USA were predominantly from
the same civilization as the older immigrants to USA. India's task of
assimilation was more complex because of the inherent differences
between ethnic groups who settled in India from ancient times. Second, Tagore pointed to the fact that in the process of assimilation,
while 'negroes [sic] remain problematic' and the American Indians
are subjected to exclusion, what was required of all immigrants and
inhabitants was complete Americanization. In the USA, in Tagore's
opinion, absorption into society was through homogenization, not
through the unification of diverse elements without doing violence
to the individuality of elements from outside; homogenization was
good for political unity but it was detrimental to the deepest instinct
of man to preserve his cultural identity, and it was 'detrimental to
the cultural diversity constituting human civilization.'[24]

These thoughts of Tagore reflect a tendency to rethink the
position he took earlier on India's unique syncretism. He is much
more acutely aware of the faultlines within the civilization. 'We
still have with us the problem of internal division....As yet we
know little of our social history....The social customs and religions
beliefs we inherit at birth obscure our vision of history. That is an
obstacle to an objective perception of reality.'[25] However, despite
these doubts, Tagore optimistically asserts his faith that the true
aim of civilization is to unify all peoples, 'what unifies humanity is
civilization.'[26]

* * *

The gospel of unity became increasingly questionable in the 1920s
and 1930s. In the last phase, between 1921 and 1941, Tagore
undergoes a painful re-thinking of his earlier notions about Indian
civilization. What is new in this phase is a scepticism about the role

of religion in Indian society, as well as doubts about the adequacy of the progress towards a syncretic unity in Indian civilization. In 1921 he writes:

We have been content with surrendering our greatest right, the right to reason and judge for ourselves, to the blind forces of shastric [scriptural] injunctions and social conventions....We refuse to eat with the Musalman, because prescribed usage is against it. In other words, we have systematically pursued a course of blind routine and habit, in which the mind has no place.[27]

This was written in course of his debate with Mahatma Gandhi; Tagore appealed to him to put on his agenda 'swaraj of the mind.'[28] In 1923–5 Tagore wrote several essays addressing the issue of disunity within a country which destroyed civilizational unity. He pointed to the rifts within the Hindu community on caste lines, and between the Hindu and Muslim communities on account of religious prejudices. He cited instances such as the uneasy relationship between the two communities in Bengal during the Swadeshi agitation, or again during the Mapilla agitation in Kerala. Later in the 1930s this theme became a dominant one in Tagore's essays. As distinct from his previous pronouncements, he now held the view that Hinduism was, from after the Buddhist era—what he called later Hinduism—was built on principles of exclusion and thus unity with others was impossible within the confines of prescriptions of religious scriptures and customs.

At one time in India Ionians [Yavanas], Persians, the Shakas and other ethnic groups had come and mingled....The Hindu age [that is, post-Buddhist era] was an age of reaction—an age when Brahminic religion was deliberately built permanently. Unsurpassable barriers of custom were erected....Hindus in India had constructed religion as a baffle-wall to eliminate admixture with and influence of external elements. Its very nature is to forbid and to reject. Nowhere in the world was ever created such a skillfully erected barrier to prevent all manner of blending. [29]

Tagore hazarded the guess that Muslims in India were also similarly circumscribed by a barrier, but that fact did not altogether govern their daily life. The only way out of this impasse, Tagore speculated, was the path shown by Europe which emerged from medievalism

to modernity through the spread of modern knowledge and
rationality. Thus Tagore, speaking like a successor to the tradition
of Enlightenment, linked the situation in India to the prospect of
a new age which will break the bonds of blind religiosity within
which Hindus and Muslim were imprisoned.[30] More pointedly,
after the assassination of Swami Shradhanand, Tagore writes: Why
are the Hindu political leaders surprised when, after centuries of
disdainful exclusion of Muslims, one day the Muslims say 'we
are separate'?[31] Later, during the Round Table Conference (1931)
which starkly revealed communal differences, Tagore writes again:
leaders of religious communities distort the sacred message of the
founders of religions and hence there develops a conflict between
religion as a system (*dharma-tantra*) and true *dharma*. This is why
'History reveals that time and again whenever a nation undergoes a
revolutionary change inspired by new ideas there develops an anti-
religious outlook.'[32] Tagore recalled the French Revolution of 1789,
the Russian Revolution of 1917, the Spanish Republicans' battle
against the Church and Kemal Ataturk's movement from 1923 in
Turkey.

In 1926 a crucial experience for Tagore was his witnessing a
huge communal riot which started in the area in Calcutta where
his ancestral home was located. The riot started in Jorasanko,
the issue being the failure of an Arya Samaj band to stop playing
musical instruments while passing a mosque at the time of azan on
2 April 1926. The police commissioner reported that from then to
9 May altogether forty-four lives were lost and 584 were injured
in the communal riot all over the city. Eventually the Staffordshire
Regiment and Section 144 of the Penal Code, forbidding all
assemblies, quelled the riots. This riot was part of a much wider
pattern of communal conflicts.[33] Between July 1925 and April
1926 such riots took place in Delhi, Allahabad, Lahore, Panipat,
Hyderabad, Bombay, Ahmedabad, and some smaller towns in
their vicinity. After the Calcutta riots there were more communal
disturbances between April and September 1926 in Rawalpindi,
Allahabad, Dacca, and Delhi. Tagore who happened to be residing

in his ancestral home in Jorasanko during the riots wrote a poem burning with anger, 'Dharma-moha'. 'Delusion disguised as faith/... Thy altar awash with blood/smash, smash that into oblivion/Strike your thunderbolt on the prison-walls around faith/And bring the light of knowledge into this benighted land.'[34] This was followed by a speech at Santiniketan which has been recorded by his colleague on the faculty of Visva-Bharti, Kshiti Mohan Sen (curiously, perhaps because it speaks of atheism, the speech was never included in the collected works of Tagore). 'Straight-forward atheism is preferable to this terrible thing, delusion of religiosity. If you do not keep your eyes shut you can see how disgusting is the satanic bestiality which wears the garb of religion ... I do not see any path other than beginning anew by burning in the fire of atheism all perversions of religion.'[35] Tagore proposed that religion is an individual's private belief, it should not form a basis for constructing a community.

The consistent critique of communalism—reaching even to a point where Tagore offered atheism as an alternative to perverse religiosity—and the recognition of the fault-lines dividing the putative national identity, obviously raised a question. If that was the state of the nation, what remained of the notion of India's civilizational unity? Tagore's answer seems to be that progress towards attaining nationhood in the European sense of the term was not necessarily progress in the evolution of civilization. 'We have for over a century been dragged by the prosperous West behind its chariot ... We agreed to acknowledge that the chariot-drive was Progress and that Progress was civilization. If we ever ventured to ask, "progress towards what, progress for whom?"—it was considered to be peculiarly and ridiculously Oriental to entertain such doubts about the absoluteness of Progress.'[36] Here and in other texts of his speeches in China in 1924 (published by him in 1925) Tagore makes a distinction between civilization as Progress from the Western point of view and civilization conceived as *dharma*. 'The word *civilization* being an European word, we have hardly taken the trouble to find out its real meaning. For over a century we have accepted it, as we may accept a gift horse....'[37] Civilization,

defined as 'the principle which holds us firm together and leads us
to our best welfare' is like *dharma* and from that principle Europe
departed in modern times. In Europe the 'ideal of civilization....
has been pushed aside by the love of Power' and by the greed
for material wealth. Tagore's writings on this theme in 1925 are
probably a little obscure—and they do show a strong resemblance
to Mahatma Gandhi's in 1909 in *Hind Swaraj*. But the critique of
European nationalism is loud and clear. Not only in his essays on
Nationalism (1921) cited earlier but in other writings around this
time the critique is often repeated. Thus, for instance, in 1922 in
essays and speeches written in North America, in *Creative Unity*:

Nationalism in the training of a whole people for a narrow ideal and
when it gets hold of their minds it is sure to lead to moral degeneracy and
intellectual blindness....It is the emphasis laid in Europe upon the idea of
the Nation's constant increase of power, which is becoming the greatest
danger to man, both in its direct activity and its power of infection....
[Men] are taught by repeated devices the lesson that the Nation is greater
than the people, while yet it scatters to the winds the moral law that the
people have held sacred.[38]

Tagore also indicts 'patriotism' when he says that the 'spirit of
national selfishness' is dangerous when it is 'decked with the
showy title of "Patriotism" proudly walks abroad, passing itself off
as a highly moral influence. Thus it has spread its inflammatory
contagion all over the world.'[39]

    In his writings in the 1930s Tagore further develops his evalua-
tion of the relationship between the Indian and Western civilizations.
In a long essay in 1933 (the title 'Kalantar' can be roughly translated
as 'New Age') he offers a historical survey of that relationship. He
begins with recalling how Europe at one time appeared to uphold
values which attracted the admiration of the best of minds in India:

We saw an endeavour to undo the wrongs human beings had suffered, we
heard in political thought the idea of unshackling mankind, we saw efforts
to stop commerce in human beings [as slaves]. We must acknowledge that
there was much that was new in these ideas. Till then we [in India] were
accustomed to accept that some human beings must accept denial of certain
right because of birth into a certain caste or the destiny of *karma* in previous

birth....Even today in our domestic interior and in our social interactions, values such as respect for the individuality of a person, right to equal treatment of equal members of society, have not been fully internalized in our culture.[40]

Tagore recalled that from the French Revolution to the Civil War in USA on the issue of abolition of slavery, the West was inspired by human values, some of which also inspired a re-awakening in Asia from the late nineteenth century. In the twentieth century Tagore, perceives a great change: Europe ceases to play the role it did earlier and this reversal of past trends came when the peoples of the colonized countries began to claim a share in the progress Europe had made as also their right of self-governance. Tagore cited the Opium Wars in China, the domination acquired over Persia, the inhuman aspects of colonial rule in Congo, a minority's stranglehold over the majority in Ireland, and, finally, the re-crudescence of Fascism in continental Europe. He ends the essay on a somewhat inconclusive note: given this course of development of a civilization once inspired a reawakening in Asia and continues to shape the modern world, is there any hope left for humanity?

In 1941 Tagore addressed this question again in the last essay he wrote before his death. This essay, *The Crisis in Civilization*, is better known because it was translated into English, but it is by and large a restatement of Tagore's thoughts in the essay of 1931 cited earlier. Jawaharlal Nehru quotes long extracts from his essay in several places in *The Discovery of India* (1946). In this essay Tagore, a successor to the Enlightenment tradition, once again recalls that at one time India had perceived in European civilization the prospect of humanity's progress. 'I had at one time believed that the springs of civilization would issue out of the heart of Europe. But today, when I am about to quit the world, that faith has gone bankrupt altogether. As I look around I see the crumbling ruins of a proud civilization strewn like a vast heap of futility.' Reflecting on the world as it emerged from World War II, he said:

From one end of the world to the other the poisonous fumes of hatred darken the atmosphere....The wheels of fate will some day compel the English to give up their Indian empire. But what kind of India will they leave behind, what stark misery? When the stream of their country's administration runs dry at last, what a waste of mud and filth they will leave behind![41]

And in the face of this crisis in civilization Tagore could only assert his faith: 'And yet I shall not commit the grievous sin of losing faith in man.'

A surprising thing about this essay of 1941 is that it comes to a sudden closure with that assertion of faith, an assertion which is quite against the grain of the argument in the entire text positing a highly negative evaluation of European civilization. To understand the declaration of faith in humanity at the end, despite all that has been said before that, one might turn to one of Tagore's more balanced pronouncements on the question. In a now forgotten address to the University of Calcutta on the occasion of its annual convocation of 1937—a text which has not been included in any of the numerous collections of Tagore's works—the issue of crisis of civilization and the possible resolution of the crisis is addressed. (This text is available only in the *Calendar of the University of Calcutta, 1938*.) That speech of 1937 has not received the attention it merits and a few quotations from that will be useful in our attempt to understand the complexities and ambiguities of the relationship between the civilization of Europe and intellectuals who observed it from their standpoint outside of it. Tagore said:

I am aware that latterly a bitter protest has gone forth from the Eastern world against the claim to greatness of European civilization and culture.... When in the beginning or middle of the Nineteenth Century we made our first acquaintance with European civilization, our joy and admiration freely went out to it in the belief that it had come into the world animated with a genuine respect for man....But, as the years went by, within the short span of our own life time, we have seen this love of humanity, this sense of justice, growing feebler and feebler, till at last there is left no civilized Court of Appeal where the plaint of the persecuted against the powerful oppressor has any chance of being heard on the ground of righteousness.[42]

At the same time, Tagore believed that all was not over with European civilization. He reminds us:

in the history and literature of this same civilization, have we not, one day, seen its true love for Man?....I will not say that the brilliance of its rise was false, and that it is the darkness of its debasement which is true. Civilization has, on many an occasion, taken false steps, proved untrue to itself, repudiated its own supreme gift to humanity. We have beheld the same unfortunate lapses in our own country, as well as outside it....Europe has provided the world with the gifts of a great culture—had it not the power to do so, it would never have attained its supremacy. It has given the example of dauntless courage, ungrudging self-sacrifice, it has shown tireless energy in the acquisition and spread of knowledge, in the making of institutions for human Welfare.[43]

Tagore goes on to recall individuals in Europe who continued to serve humanity; probably he had in mind friends like C.F. Andrews and W.W. Pearson:

Even these days of its self-abasement, there are still before us its true representatives who are ready to suffer punishment in their fearless protest against its iniquities, in their chivalrous championship of its victims....The inspiration that holds them steadfast to their best instincts, through all the outrage and degeneracy around them, that inspiration is the truth dwelling in the heart of Western civilization. It is from that we have to learn, not from the disastrous self-degradation of the modern Western nations.[44]

* * *

We have tried to understand Tagore's highly complex contribution to the discourse of civilization. Over a period of six decades he intervened intermittently in that discourse and his approach underwent some changes as we have noticed above. What were his specific contributions? First, it seems that he was one of the first— if not the first—to develop the concept of 'syncretism' in Indian civilization. The notion he put forward in 1902 that in Indian civilization there was a tendency to assimilate diversities to establish unity—a notion which he poetically expressed in the first stanza of a poem which was eventually to become the Indian national anthem—exceeded the boundaries of earlier statements about the geographical unity of the Indian subcontinent. The concept of a 'syncretic civilization' proved to be in later times a main plank of the nationalist construction of Indian unity, even if nationhood in the European sense of the term was yet to be attained. The concept of syncretism was needed to establish an idea of civilizational unity.

Second, in postulating a generic difference between the state-centred civilization of Europe and the civilization of India where *samaja* or society was given centrality, Tagore made a rather new, though perhaps debatable, point. In the absence of continuity through a territorially definable political unit, there was a need for such a postulate. The continuity of the Indian civilization over millennia was a vital element in nationalist imagination of India's past, but such a continuity could only reside in the society and culture of the people, there was no political entity that survived for that length of time. A socio-cultural continuity was a surrogate for a political-territorial continuity.

Third, unlike many of his contemporaries, Tagore perceived the limitations of nationalism, which he identified as a thing European in origin, as an ideology of aggrandizement on a global scale, and as a model unworthy of emulation for Indians. Nehru commented on this in his *The Discovery of India* when he said: 'Nationalism is a narrowing creed, and nationalism in conflict with dominating imperialism produces all manner of frustrations and complexes. It was Tagore's immense service to India, as it has been Gandhi's in a different plane, that he forced the people in some measure out of their narrow grooves of thought and made them think of broader issues affecting humanity.'[45]

Finally, Tagore was also, towards the end of his life, a forthright critic of that society which he earlier elevated to a central place in the evolution of Indian civilization as a unity. Tagore saw in that society, in the light of rising communalism from 1920s onwards, fault-lines which threatened the 'syncretic' civilization he postulated decades ago. He saw in that society elements such as casteism, communalism and purblind traditionalism which were impediments to the unity and progress of the Indian people. Tagore began to interrogate the postulate of syncretism he had propagated earlier and found the reality around him in India different from what his earlier assumptions would lead one to believe. At the same time, in the broader perspective of human civilization as a whole, he perceived a crisis in civilization. Tagore recognized how the promise his generation had once seen in Europe's message of Progress for humanity met with disillusionment in the early decades of the twentieth century.[46]

NOTES

1. Jawaharlal Nehru, *The Discovery of India* (Signet Press, Calcutta, 1946; John Day, New York, 1946).

2. Rabindranath Tagore, *Crisis in Civilization* (Calcutta: Visva-Bharati, 1941, reprint 1964).

3. Tagore writes thus just twenty years after the uprising of 1857 when the memory of the uprising was still fresh as far as the elders of the family were concerned; Rabindranath's father Debendranath was caught in the turmoil of 1857 in north India and has left a vivid account in his memoirs.

4. Bankimchandra Chatterjee, 'Banglar Itihas Sambandhe Koyekti Katha' (A Few Words Concerning the History of Bengal), *Bangadarshan*, 1281 BS (1874); in *Bankim Rachanavali*, (ed.) J.C. Bagal (Sahitya Samsad, Calcutta, 1959), vol. II, pp. 336–40.

5. Rabindranath Tagore, 'Aitihasik Chitra' (Images from History), *Itihas* (Visva-Bharati, Calcutta, 1955), p. 140.

6. Rabindranath Tagore, 'Bharatvarsher Itihas' (The History of India), *Bangadarshan*, 1309 BS (1902) revised and reprinted in 1905 and 1908; vide *Itihas*, p. 7.

7. Ibid., p. 9.

8. Ibid., pp. 8–9.

9. Ibid., pp. 10–11.

10. Rabindranath Tagore, 'Bharatvarsher Itihaser Dhara' (The Course of Indian History), English translation by Sir Jadu Nath Sarkar under the title, 'A Vision of Indian History', *The Modern Review*, August–September 1913; *Itihas*, pp. 16–59.

11. Ibid., p. 13.

12. Andrew Robinson and Krishna Dutta (eds), *Rabindranath Tagore: The Myriad-minded Man* (Bloomsbury, London, 1996), chapter 21.

13. Rabindranath Tagore, *Nationalism* (ed.) E.P. Thompson (Papermac, London, 1992).

14. Rabindranath Tagore, *Nationalism* (in English), in *The English Writings of Rabindranath Tagore* (ed.) Sisir Kumar Das (Sahitya Academi, Delhi, 1996; first published by Macmillan, New York, 1917) vol. II, p. 440.

15. Tagore, *Nationalism* (ed.) Das, p. 426.

16. Ibid., pp. 426–7.

17. Ibid., p. 428.

18. Ibid., p. 456.

19. Ibid., p. 457.

20. Ibid., p. 459.

21. Ibid, pp. 459–62.

22. Tagore, *Itihas*, p. 80.

23. 'Bharat Itihas Charcha' (The Study of Indian History), 1919, in his *Itihas*, p. 80.

24. Ibid., pp. 80–1.

25. Ibid., pp. 81–2.

26. Ibid., p. 79.

27. Tagore, 'The Call of Truth' (English translation) in Bhattacharya (ed.), *The Mahatma and the Poet*, p. 76.

28. Tagore, 'Striving for Swaraj', (English translation) in Bhattacharya (ed.), *The Mahatma and the Poet*, pp. 113–21.

29. Tagore, 'Hindu Musalman' (The Hindus and the Muslims) (1931), *Itihas*, p. 313.

30. Ibid., p. 314.

31. Tagore, 'Swami Shradhananda' (1926), ibid., pp. 315–22.

32. Tagore, 'Hindu Musalman' (1931), ibid., p. 325

33. On the 1926 riot and Tagore's reaction, I draw upon sources in Sabyasachi Bhattacharya, 'The Archeology of a Poem', *The Telegraph*, Calcutta, 20 August 1993.

34. 'Dharma-moha', *Parishesh*, *Rabindra Rachanabali* (Vishwa-Bharati, Santiniketan), vol. VIII, p. 206; The Vice Chancellor of Visva-Bharati made this poem the theme of his Foundation Day Address at Santiniketan a few days after the demolition of Babri Mosque in December 1992.

35. See note 32 earlier, and Tagore to Nirmal Kumari Mahalanobis, 24 January 1927, Gorachand Saha (ed.), *Rabindra Patrabali* (Visva-Bharati, Calcutta, 1984), p. 252.

36. Rabindranath Tagore, *Talks in China* (1925), in Das (ed.), *The English Writings of Rabindranath Tagore*, p. 622.

37. Ibid., p. 621.

38. Tagore, 'The Nation', in *Creative Unity*, in S.K. Das (ed.), *The English Writings of Rabindranath Tagore*, p. 549.

39. Ibid., p. 551.

40. Tagore, 'Kalantar' (New Age), in *Kalantar* (Visva-Bharati Publications, Calcutta, 1937), pp. 17–18.

41. Tagore, *Crisis in Civilization*.

42. Rabindranath Tagore, *Convocation Address at the University of Calcutta* (Calcutta University Press, Calcutta, 1937), pp. 11–12.

43. Ibid., p. 13.

44. Ibid., p. 14.

45. Nehru, *Discovery of India*, p. 342.

46. Tagore, *Convocation Address*.

CHAPTER 4

Discovering and Inventing India

Jawaharlal Nehru

We are so familiar with the representation of India as a great civilization which brings about unity amidst diversities, and accommodates in the Indian polity a pluralistic society, that we take the Indian discourse of civilization for granted. This is especially true of the decades since independence. How mistaken we may be in taking that conception for granted becomes obvious when we look at some other Third World countries where such an accommodative concept of civilization is not the generally accepted currency of the realm. In the task of installing the conceptual approach to India's civilization as it had developed in the nationalist discourse and to try to make it a foundational idea in the agenda of state building in the post-colonial period, Jawaharlal Nehru played a very important role. Shortly before India attained independence Nehru grappled with the issue in *The Discovery of India,* written while he was in the Ahmedabad Fort Jail.[1]

This work was written in 1944, published in 1946 and then revised several times while it underwent four editions from 1946–56. Nehru reminded himself and his reader that the book was written 'in the close and abnormal atmosphere of prison' and went on to add: 'It is mine and not wholly mine, as I am constituted today; it represents rather some past self of mine which had already joined that long succession of other selves that existed for a while and faded away, leaving only a memory behind.'[2] He adds in the closing pages in a rather self-conscious manner: 'I have covered a thousand hand-written paper with this jumble of ideas in my mind.... I have traveled in the past and peeped into the future.'[3] Nehru's official biographer wrote later in a rather critical vein: 'This is a great jumble of a book which bears the marks of haste and tension,' and 'lacking in analysis, elegance and clear thinking'; it 'carried not a precise, scientific argument but a buoyant message.'[4] Be that as it may, the book was a great success and was probably the only 'best-seller' the author produced. The reason why it appealed to a vast readership was, first, that it was published about the time when India attained independence; the book addressed the question, what was Nehru's idea of India's civilization as a guide to her post-independence future.

In a significant statement made casually, Nehru wrote in 1942: 'I was a child of Asia, with her tradition in my blood, and with pride in her past and faith in her future, and I was foster-child of the Western World, knowing it fairly well and appreciating its great achievements.'[5] *The Discovery of India* may be read as a product of such a mind. A constant search for the traditions he spoke of and likewise a search for a civilizational strand in historiography is evident in Nehru's letters and writings from the 1930s. Nehru's enquiry into India's civilization in *The Discovery of India* was preceded by a long intellectual preparation. For instance, in 1930 when he was in jail, he tried hard to get the recently translated volumes of Oswald Spengler's *Decline of the West.* He says that his jailors suspected that 'it contained something subversive of the British Government.'[6] In the prison letters and diaries of 1930 there are not less than half-a-dozen references to Spengler's work—which he eventually obtained and read thoroughly. Similarly, while he served another prison term in 1932, we find him immersed in the historian Rene Grouset's book on *The Civilization of India*.[7] While pursuing his interest in the history of Indian civilization, Nehru distanced himself from those who were intent on just glorifying India's past. He writes in 1934, again from jail, of the Indian habit of endowing 'the ancients with every virtue under the sun', and depicting 'a golden age when the land flowed with milk and honey.'[8] What immediate reason led Nehru to write *The Discovery of India* is not recorded, but this was the intellectual background leading to that enterprise.

This eloquent and imaginative exposition of the nationalist stance on the issue of civilization was published at a poignant moment when the victory of the nationalist struggle was imminent and at the same time, the unity nationalists had upheld as an inheritance from Indian civilization was about to be challenged successfully and Partition seemed to be inevitable in the predictable future.

The civilizational unity of India is a major theme in this work. Nehru begins the book with the question, 'What is this India, apart from her physical and geographical aspects?'[9] He ends the work with reflections on the same question in the last chapter: India is 'a cultural unity amidst diversity, a bundle of contradictions held together by strong but invisible threads....She is a myth and an idea, a dream and a vision, and yet very real and present and pervasive.'[10] The idea that India was held together by bonds of unity rooted in the past of Indian civilization was, as I have said not altogether new for it was the theme of one or two earlier writers including Rabindranath Tagore and Mahatma Gandhi. What was new in Nehru's statement was the political relevance of that message in the context of the 1940s. Neither Tagore in 1902 nor Gandhi in 1909 was writing in the context of the political polarization which oppressed Nehru's mind. Given the widening communal divide the Partition of August 1947 was foreseeable when Nehru wrote

The Discovery of India. In this context Nehru's effort to appeal
to the history of Indian civilization has a different significance. He
repeatedly reverts to the theme of India's unity amidst diversity. I
shall cite only one or two such passages. He says over and again that
despite ethnic diversity and differences in religious belief systems
the people of India, 'have been throughout the ages distinctively
Indian, with the same national heritage.'[11] He goes on to say;
'Disruptive tendencies gave rise immediately to an attempt to find a
synthesis. Some kind of a dream of unity has occupied the mind of
India since the dawn of civilization.' It was a dream that included
'the widest tolerance of belief and custom.'[12] Nehru acknowledges
that this perception is coloured by nationalism, that it was a
perception 'conditioned and limited in many ways. It took the form
of nationalism....But nationalism was and is inevitable in India of
my day.'[13] There is a poignancy in the fact that Nehru, on the eve of
the moment India would be divided, writes of India as 'a myth' and
'yet very real'.[14] The unity which Tagore in 1902 or Gandhi in 1909
wrote of confidently as an enduring fact of Indian history, Nehru
writes of as a *dream,* although it is also 'in some ways a reality'.
That is the difference between the perspective of the first decade of
the twentieth century and that of the 1940s when Nehru wrote of
India's civilizational unity.

* * *

Although *The Discovery of India* did not, as Nehru's official
biographer Gopal has pointed out, contain very many original
ideas in respect of Indian civilization there is considerable charm in
the free-floating succession of images and thoughts. And precisely
because the author could not access scholarly works in jail, the
style is almost conversational, unburdened with many references
and citations. However, careful readers might discern three major
strands of thought which drive the main argument and run through
the entire book. First, there is a sense of wonder, what accounts for
the continuity and the enduring quality of India's civilizations for
several millennia. Second, there is a robust hypothesis about India's

ability to synthesize diversities into a unity. Third, Nehru denounces a tendency to glorify the past and at the same time he is critical of the modern tendency to reject that ancient past; as he put it once, we cannot live without a past but at the same time we cannot live in the past.

The first of these issues is posited in the first few pages. 'Astonishing thought that any culture or civilization should have ...continuity for five or six thousand years or more....[India's] cultural basis was strong enough to endure. What was the secret of this strength?'[15] Nehru reflects that there was 'something unique about the continuity of a cultural tradition' in India—'only China had such a continuity of tradition.'[16] Nehru cited authors like Max Müller and Gordon Childe who commented on this continuity. He also thought that the influence of Indian civilization on other parts of the world, specially Southeast Asia, was an evidence of the strength of Indian's civilization; he cited Rabindranath Tagore's rhetorical reference to the so-called colonies in South East Asia: 'To know my country one has to travel to that age, when she... transcended her physical boundaries, when she revealed her being in a radiant magnanimity which illumined the eastern horizon... and not now when she has withdrawn herself into a narrow barrier of obscurity, into a miserly pride of exclusiveness, into a narrow poverty of mind....'[17]

The second recurring idea in Nehru's text is that Indian civilization was syncretist. 'The diversity of India is tremendous; it is obvious; it lies on the surface and anybody can see it. It concerns itself with physical appearances as well as with certain mental habits and traits.'[18] And yet, he went on to argue,

Ancient India, like ancient China, was a world in itself, a culture and a civilization which gave shape to all things. Foreign influences poured in and often influenced that culture and were absorbed. Disruptive tendencies gave rise immediately to an attempt to find a synthesis....That unity was not conceived as something imposed from outside, a standardization of externals or even of beliefs. It was something deeper and, within its fold, the widest tolerance of belief and custom was practised and every variety acknowledged and even encouraged.[19]

Then Nehru describes his political tours through the length and breadth of India, the variousness of the country, and also what he perceived as the common 'culture of the masses.'[20] This idea of India's syncretic unity no doubt received a blow in the Partition of 1947, but Nehru continued to assert that proposition. For instance, his Address to the Indian Science Congress in 1953: 'India has had that past tradition of synthesis....Currents came to it, rivers of humanity flowed into it, and got mixed up with the ocean of India, making changes there no doubt, and affecting it and being affected by it. And through this course of ages India of today, grew up....And even though I might be a politician overwhelmed with the problems of the day, I cannot help, as no sensitive person can, looking a little beyond today, a little beyond tomorrow even, for then, my own country's history pursues me....'[21] Another instance is an essay to introduce a book by the eminent Hindi author Ramdhari Sinha 'Dinkar' in 1955:

> We must endeavour to understand what India is and how this nation has developed its composite personality with its many facets and yet with an enduring unity. No one section of the community in India can lay claim to the sole possession of the mind and thought of India....If I look at India I find...the gradual growth of a composite culture of the Indian people.... [T]his national culture gradually grew and took shape. It had a remarkable capacity for synthesis and of absorbing new elements. So long as it did so it was dynamic and living. In later years it lost the dynamic quality and became essentially static which led to weakness in all fields....Today we face the same problem in a different context. There are powerful forces working for unity, not only political but cultural also. There are also forces that disrupt and lay stress on separateness. The question, therefore, for us today is not an academic one but a vital issue on the understanding of which depends our future.[22]

Thus Nehru, reading the past in the light of his own times, repeatedly emphasized what he perceived as the syncretic nature of India's civilization through history.

This reading can be construed as a false claim to a unique and glorious past. Nehru shows a measure of intellectual honesty in disclaiming that. He did not want to claim that India was unique in possessing an old culture among nations since each country is unique among its own kind.[23] There he differed from the Gandhian position, as of 1909 in *Hind Swaraj*. In *The Discovery of India* Nehru was critical of 'this looking back to the past and finding comfort and sustenance there'; he recalled that unlike his followers,

Vivekananda himself was careful to warn his people not to dwell too much on the past, but to look to the future. 'When, O Lord', he wrote, 'shall our land be free from this eternal dwelling upon the past?' But he himself and others had evoked that past and there was glamour in it, and no getting away from it.[24]

He recognized periods of decline in all civilization, an idea he might have developed from his study of Edward Gibbon and Oswald Spengler. India, he maintained, went through such a period of decline towards the end of the first millennium AD and he cites S. Radhakrishnan and Sylvain Levi's views that India suffered a kind of cultural stagnation and loss of creativity.[25] In a long passage on the collapse of the Roman empire, Nehru compared that decline with India's historical experience. One of the factors in India contributing to the civilizations continuity was, he thought, was the fact that the caste system which gave an 'amazing stability to Indian civilization.' But at the same time the caste system 'carried within it the seeds of destruction.'[26] (Similar views were expressed by Tagore and D.D. Kosambi.) Nehru saw the seeds of destruction in the stasis enforced by the caste system, the restriction on mobility due to a hereditary occupational structure, and the consequent tendency 'to confine oneself to the old groove, to restrict initiative and the spirit of innovation.'

Thus Nehru clearly distanced himself from those nationalist thinkers who tended to idealize the Indian past. His aim seems to be to strike a balance: he writes that a blind reverence for the past is bad so also is a contempt for it, for no future can be founded on either of these—and one must look to the future. [27] He wrote thus in 1944 and this became a running theme in his pronouncements after 1947 when he was at the helm of affairs. We may note his interest in museums: New Delhi, he said, was a city without a soul and when Independence came Delhi did not even have a museum to serve as a window into the past. Such a window was needed, he believed, to look out towards the broader and richer and deeper things of life. [28] He was perhaps the first to give attention to the artifices of *representation*. His object of projecting India's past to impress upon the public mind Indian history as he conceived it is in evidence in the selection of certain symbols for the new Republic of India, for example, the Ashoka pillar which he installed in the National Museum and the Buddhist wheel of *dharma,* later known as the Asoka *chakra.* Likewise, an imaginative appropriation of fragments of the past is exemplified in his interest in museums and specially the creation of the National Museum in Delhi at a central place, a permanent reminder of the heritage of an ancient civilization, in the face of the British representation of imperial might in the monumental India Gate.

* * *

Nehru was dissatisfied with 'the type of history we read' which often consists of 'a string of events, of battles and of kings, which cannot possibly inspire anybody.'[29] In fact there were indeed very few works of Indian history which gave centrality to the civilization of India in the manner Nehru did in *The Discovery of India.* He confided to his friend K.M. Panikkar his despair with the abysmally poor quality of Indian academic history writing. In fact in the pre-independence period the nationalist cause was poorly served by the average academic output in historiography. The universities and undergraduate colleges offered teaching on lines approved by governing bodies which were controlled by government nominees. The textbooks were those approved by committees of the same kind and most often the committees privileged books written by British authors who had failed to make it in the universities in England. Even if Indian authors ventured to write they would 'have to step carefully to keep to the line laid down by text book committees and a notion of loyalty to the Raj.'[30] That description by Tagore was fairly accurate and it accounts for the quality of academic writing Nehru complained of.

Who then gave expression, in the early half of the twentieth century, to the nationalist urge to rewrite history and to recover the Indian voice in interpreting India's culture and civilization? We have to go back into the past to answer this question. They were writers of books of history, mainly regional history, who did not belong to the ranks of professional historians. The hunger for history also led to the creation of many organizations for the collection of historical sources and cultural artifacts, and for promotion of historical research and publication. These organizations and amateur historians were often linked with the nationalist leaders and the Indian National Congress. While lending support to the national cause, as they saw it in their light, their own base of support was regional. They drew support from regional identity consciousness and this was reflected in their drive to write regional or local history. It will be useful to look at, below the highly visible level of a Tagore or a Nehru, some representative figures who engaged in that agenda at the regional level.

Maharashtra, endowed with a rich historical literature in the form of *bakhar*s, saw the development of regional historical studies much earlier than other regions. A.R. Kulkarni and Richard P. Tucker have provided a detailed history of the 'archival movement' in late nineteenth and early twentieth century Bombay Presidency. The 'archival movement' was an effort on the part of intellectuals to preserve historical records and to make them available to historians; archiving also gave rise to a new interpretative approach to Maratha history. Among the main champions of the movement were V.K. Rajwade (1863–1926) and Mahadev Govind Ranade (1842–1901) and two major organizations involved were Bharatiya Itihas Samsodhak Mandal and the Deccan Vernacular Translation Society. The role played by M.G. Ranade was very important because he was also a prominent nationalist spokesman in public life. He was a founder of the Widow Remarriage Association (1861) and the Deccan Education Society (1884) as well as a staunch supporter of the Indian National Congress from its first session (1885) in Bombay, and a leading member of a parallel Social Reform

Conference in tandem with each session of the Congress. A brilliant lawyer, he eventually became a judge at Bombay High Court and his special area being revenue law, he pioneered Indians' explorations in Indian economy and economic history.

The first battle faced by the archival movement of Rajwade and Ranade was to pressure the Bombay Government to open the archives, especially the Peshwa *daftar* records at Poona, to scholarly research. The resistance of the government to allowing free access to the historical records kept under the control of British officials in the Alienation Office, Revenue Department, was very strong in the 1890s and continued to be so till the 1930s. The officials were anxious about the wisdom of providing material which may be 'used against government either politically or otherwise.'[31] Further, there were in official circles apprehensions about opening the archives to 'frivolous and impertinent writers, unscrupulous journalists' who might misuse the opportunity with results 'disastrous to the government.'[32]

Ranade, as President of the Deccan Vernacular Translation Society, secured in 1897 permission of the government to publish selections from Peshwa's records.[33] Even though Ranade's Vernacular Translation Society was allowed to publish selections from Peshwa's records, the text and annotations were subject to official scrutiny before publication. An 'Introduction to the Peshwa's Diaries' written by Ranade was excluded from the volume that was published in 1901. The government's view was that Ranade's 'Introduction' was 'really an essay written with the object of exhibiting the rule of the Marathas in the most favourable light possible and is coloured throughout with the personal opinion and bias of the author.'[34] Ranade's essay was published separately and not as part of this government approved selection of records it was intended to introduce. The main contribution Ranade made as a historian was his work on the *Rise of the Maratha Power*, originally a series of essays written between 1893 and 1900 and published in a book form shortly before Ranade passed away in 1901.[35]

Ranade's history of the rise of the Marathas is presented by him in a prefatory statement as a 'history from the Indian standpoint.' Perhaps because he apprehended that it might be read as an anti-British tract, Ranade added that his object was to persuade the 'representatives of the conquering British power' to be just to the 'departed great whose names are cherished by millions in India.' The subject of the narrative in Ranade's book, however, was clearly a critique of Grant Duff. *History of the Mahrattas* (1826) by Grant Duff was a textbook in Bombay Presidency for decades and it was reprinted many times (the reprints of 1861, 1873, 1878, 1912, 1921 are known, but there may have been more reprints). Grant Duff made in 1819 the first attempt to collect in Poona old *sanads, kaifyats, watanpatras*, and other material. Thus his claim to being an authority in Maratha history was strong. But Indian reaction was adverse to many of his judgements, like his claim that Shivaji 'always preferred deceit to open force', that 'duplicity and meanness are ... conspicuous in his actions'.[36] Generally Indian critics pointed to the absence in Grant Duff of the slightest recognition of the patriotic motives of the founders of Maratha power. Grant Duff's work attracted attention because it was a textbook in both English and Hindi version from 1870 in schools and colleges.[37]

Ranade's originality was that he shifted the focus of attention in the narrativization and explication of the growth of Maratha power from the purely political domain to the cultural roots of Maratha regeneration and state formation and expansion. Such an approach, he said, was needed to correct the earlier histories, including Grant Duff's, which in a narrower perspective presented the rise of Maratha power as fortuitous, solely the consequence of the actions of one personality and the immediate political circumstances. As distinct from the earlier approach, Ranade underlined the unity of the Maratha people, the culture of 'toleration and moderation' as evinced in the mobility of Shudras to higher social structure as Kshatriyas or Vaishyas, the elevation of spiritual teachers of lower castes or out-castes to widely acclaimed sainthood, and the moderating influence of local culture on 'even the Mahomedans [who] lose their bigoted character' in Maratha country. Ranade contends that Shivaji had 'mixed on equal terms with Tukaram, Ramdas and other religious teachers of his time'; what is more, for about three centuries before that people of Marathas were deeply influenced by 'preachers, both Brahman and non-Brahman, [who] were calling on people to identify Ram with Rahim, and ensure their freedom from bonds of formal ritualism and caste distinctions....'[38] In an oft-cited passage Ranade attributes to Ramdas an exhortation to Shivaji to uphold 'the duty or *Dharma* of a great rashtra or united nation.'

Thus Ranade saw in the rise of Maratha power, 'the first beginnings of what one may well call the process of nation-making.' In this fairly qualified statement, Ranade possibly meant to say that the beginnings of the nation in the making in India were inherent in the patriotic sentiments one see at work in the seventeenth century among the Marathas. The context of the statement is that Ranade is emphasizing the fact that there was an 'upheaval of the whole population, strongly bound together by the affinities of language, race, religion and literature' which led to a common aspiration for further 'solidarity by a common independent political existence.' Ranade seems to suggest that it was 'national' in that the entire population was involved, 'all classes cooperated.'[39] At the same time, he is careful to distinguish the circumstances from the process of European nation formation: 'As a first effort it was wanting in that solidity of structure which has characterised the great European nations, but there can be no mistake about this being its essential and distinguishing feature.'[40] It is therefore difficult to accept Richard Tucker's criticism that 'Ranade was faced with severe difficulties' in the face of a dilemma 'of regional versus all India nationality'.[41] Ranade looks upon regional sentiments of patriotism of nationality as the first stage marking the beginnings of Indian nationhood. Tucker is right in his assertion that in the text little or no distinction is made between the terms 'race', 'nationality' and 'nation'; but we have to bear in mind the fact that Ranade was writing for a popular readership and that these distinctions came late into the lexicon of newly developing social sciences. In popular parlance at that time those terms were often used as synonyms.

A junior contemporary of Ranade was Akshay Kumar Maitreya (1861–1930), a lawyer like Ranade, who began almost a cultural movement in Bengal to raise historical consciousness and to recover the Indian voice in an area of Indian historiography dominated by colonial historians. In his memoirs he writes that in college his syllabus of study included texts like Macaulay's essays on Robert Clive and Warren Hastings. 'While studying the text books almost every day I entered into disputes with the teacher Principal Dowding. In order to refute Macaulay's account I used to search for contrary evidence.'[42] Maitreya was one of the founders of the first historical research society organized by 'natives'—as distinct from say the Asiatic Society which was controlled by Englishmen, mainly those in the Indian Civil Service with a historical interest. Maitreya was also admitted as a member to the Asiatic Society of Calcutta and its journal carried many of his papers on inscriptions and copper plates of early medieval Bengal. As the founder Director of the Varendra Research Society from 1910 to 1930 he collected regional records, folklore, epigraphs, and related material. Eventually that effort led to the foundation of the Varendra Research Museum in 1919. Twice, successively, Maitreya launched journals of popular history in the Bengali language but the market was not large enough to recover the publication expenses. However, his works of history sold well and he was well-regarded among those readers who admired the nationalist spirit in his writings. He attended at least one session of the Indian National Congress in 1901, but it is not known whether he attended more. [43]

The most well known of these writings was Maitreya's book on Sirajuddaula, the Nawab of Bengal who besieged and captured the British fort and settlement of Calcutta in 1756 and lost Bengal to the British, in alliance with traitors in the Nawab's camp, in the battle of Plassey in 1757.[44] This work was published in 1898, about the time when Ranade was publishing his essays in Shivaji and the rise of the Marathas. Maitreya's book was designed as a defence of Sirajuddaula who was a unique object of hatred among the British of those times. Among many misdeeds attributed to him by British historians and polemicists the so-called Black Hole tragedy figured most prominently. Maitreya questioned the evidence produced in that polemical literature by contemporaries as well as by historians who came later. Not only in Maitreya's time but even later the Black Hole was to a good number of the British in India a symbol and reminder of horrible things natives were prone to do—but for firm-handed British rule. On the other hand to many Indians it was an ingenious story invented by a man called J.Z. Holwell as a means of avenging the humiliation of surrendering Calcutta to a native ruler. The defense of Sirajuddaula from the charge of perpetrating the Black Hole crime was comparable in importance to the defence of Shivaji in respect of the death of Afzal Khan. The Black Hole story remained a contentious bit of history right up to the time of Subhas Chandra Bose who put on the agenda of the Congress the demolition of a 'Black Hole Memorial', a monument erected by the British who loyally believed Holwell's story. That was as late as the 1920s. In 1890s when Maitreya wrote his refutation of the Black Hole story few Indians dared question it in public. A contemporary of Maitreya, the historian S.C. Hill contested Maitreya's views and so did Rushbrook Williams of Allahabad University. The lone British historian who by and large agreed with Maitreya on the question of the 'Black Hole' was J.H. Little of the Calcutta Historical Society. The Anglo-Indian newspapers like *The Statesman* and *The Pioneer* were, needless to say, very vocal against Maitreya. Rabindranath Tagore was one of his defenders.

The contentions around the details of the debate on the 'Black Hole' need not detain us, nor the empirically rich narrative in Maitreya's work on Sirajuddaula—we are concerned more with the agenda he addressed and the impact his attempt to re-write history created. Maitreya contended that the 'gigantic hoax of Holwell is recorded in every text-book as an actual event of history, and we have to teach it and generation after generation have to

learn it by heart.'[45] He also contested numerous statements about
the Nawab in the writings of British historians—among them he
held in high regard only two, Orme and H.S. Beveridge. Maitreya
cited their relatively unbiased views and he depended heavily on
the evidence he gathered from contemporary Muslim chroniclers.
He represented Sirajuddaula as 'unjustly condemned' by almost all
British historians. Maitrya argued that Sirajuddaula had 'tried to
stem the current of history' which carried a set of foreign merchants
to entrench themselves as rulers, and that his failure was due to
'flaws in our national character' which enabled the foreigners to
exploit the state of disunity in Bengal and to win over to their side
traitorous elements.[46] Maitreya's writings have not a trace of Hindu
prejudice against Muslim rulers, though he conceded that there was
not only political disintegration but also a 'moral degeneration'
since the decline and fall of the Mughal empire.

The significance of the role of Ranade or Maitreya was brought
out very well by Rabindranath Tagore in the three review essays he
wrote in 1898–9 on Maitreya's works. Tagore mentions historians
like Sir Alfred Lyall and lesser authors such as Sir Roper Lethbridge
and says their histories are chronicles of the machinery of government, 'human beings are absent.'[47] Moreover the British accounts of
India often contain 'imaginative untruths and exaggerations about
Indian religions, society and national character....We are compelled
to read as texts these calumnies...and learn them by heart to pass
examinations.' The great merit of works like Maitreya's, Tagore
said, was that they showed that those British authors could also
be questioned, that their evidence could be subjected to critical examination, that the British authors were not necessarily authorities.

The other point Tagore made was that in India there had
developed a new historical consciousness.

In recent years in the Bengali literary world a historical consciousness has
developed....Nowadays in the whole of India a new energy has been at
work...and a hunger for history is one of its natural consequences. This
shows that the movement led by the Congress etc. is not to dismissed as
something apart [from the cultural domain]. Sometimes I have a feeling that

all that effort each year to place before the rulers of the Raj submissions with monotonous regularity is fruitless.[48]

But the new hunger for history brought it home to him that the Congress's efforts had not been fruitless, for the Congress had been 'casting abroad the seed of certain ideas....We shall now liberate our history from alien hands and look at our Bharatvarsha in the light of our independent judgement....' [49]

It is impossible to miss one aspect of the work of M.G. Ranade, Akshay Kumar Maitreya and their peers who developed and promoted historical consciousness at the regional level. Nehru's was a discovery of India was, he himself wrote, as that of 'a foster child of the Western world.'[50] Ranade and Maitreya were far from being identified with that world, their engagement with the Indian past was from a very indigenist point of view. There was a complementarity between these two approaches, but they were different in temper and tenor of these voices talking back to their colonial interlocutors. That is the point of presenting these two approaches in this chapter.

* * *

In Nehru's times Vivekananda (1863–1902) was a formative influence on the educated public mind. Nehru mentions and quotes Vivekananda quite often in *The Discovery of India*.[51] In 1893 M.G. Ranade began to write his famous series of essays on the rise of Maratha power and about that time Akshay Kumar Maitreya began publishing his essays on the history of Bengal. In 1893 Vivekananda (1863–1902) appeared in the forum of the Parliament of Religions in Chicago and thus began a brief but brilliant career as a *sannyasin* in the public sphere, an exponent of India's ancient civilization and spiritual heritage. Arguably this Hindu sannyasin did more to push his people away from the bonds of traditional stasis than many other thinkers of his times. Nehru specially emphasized the fact that Vivekananda 'laid repeated stress on reason', for had he not said 'Experience is the only source of knowledge', and warned against the tendency 'to deliver your reason into the hands of priests.'[52]

Vivekananda to Nehru was a kind of link between the past of India and the present. As regards the theme we address in this book, there are perhaps three issues in Vivekananda's thoughts on Indian civilization which need to be addressed. Was India 'spiritual' as opposed to the materialistic West? Did India need to learn from the West? What kind of unity was possible, given the prevailing religious diversity?

Vivekananda's views on Indian civilization were somewhat different from what one would expect of a person usually described as 'spiritual'. No doubt he did often describe Indian civilization as a spiritual one, as opposed to a materialistic civilization. Thus, for instance, he writes in an essay on 'The Historical Evolution of India': 'In ancient India the centres of national life were always the intellectual and spiritual, and not political....political and social power has been always subordinated to spiritual and intellectual [power].'[53] But generally he added a qualification: there is need for a balance between the spiritual and material domains. Thus, he writes in 1896, 'A nation which is great in the possession of material power thinks that that is all to be coveted, that that is all that is meant by progress....On the other hand, another nation may think that mere material civilization is utterly useless.' The aim should be, he said, 'the harmonizing, the mingling of these two ideals.'[54] Those who 'apotheosise the material world into a God' are wrong, 'yet, perhaps some sort of materialism, toned down by our own requirements, would be a blessing to many of our brothers who are not yet rise for the highest truths.'[55] Many who claim to be 'spiritual' are degraded representatives of a tradition that is scarcely alive: 'we are neither Vedantists, most of us now, nor Pauranics, nor Tantrics. We are just "don't-touchists". Our religion is in the kitchen, our religion is "don't touch me, I am holy".'[56] Thus, he did not set much store by the Indian claim to spirituality. Moreover, he stated in a seminar at the Graduate Philosophical Society of Harvard University in 1896, his belief that 'Civilization is the manifestation of divinity in man.'[57] This was in answer to a question from the floor, 'what is the Vedantic idea of civilization?' That put a different spin on

the meaning of spirituality in a civilization. One notices that on
the whole Vivekananda tended to give less weight to the notion of
Indian 'spirituality' when his interlocutors were Indians than he did
when he spoke to or wrote for a Western audience. This was because
he had his doubts about Indians' tendency to claim spirituality. And
he undoubtedly looked upon the spiritual–materialistic dichotomy
as too simplistic.

The second major feature of Vivekananda's approach to the
notion of civilization is that he was critical of many features of
India's society and culture and was willing to concede that India
had to learn a good deal from the West. Jawaharlal Nehru quotes
Vivekananda's critique:

He condemned occultism and mysticism...those creepy things, there may
be great truths in them, but they have nearly destroyed us....go back to
your Upanishads...and part from all these mysterious things, all these
weakening things....I would rather see everyone of you rank atheists than
superstitious fools, for the atheist is alive and you can make something of
him. But if superstition enters...degradation has seized upon the life. So
Vivekananda thundered from Cape Comorin on the southern tip of India to
the Himalayas, and he wore himself out in the process, dying in 1902 when
he was 39 years of age.[58]

It is not surprising that Nehru was impressed with this part of
Vivekananda's message for he said such things over and again. Apart
from his critical attitude to Indian society as it was in his days;
Vivekananda also anticipated Nehru's line of thinking in preaching
India's need to learn from Western civilization, without getting into
the trap of mistaking imitation of the West as an adequate substitute
for internalization of the values at the core of Western civilization.
In the very first essay he wrote in 1899 in the opening number of
his Bengali journal Udbodhan, he spoke of the need to reconcile
the West with the East: in remote antiquity India and Greece, two
of the earliest streams of civilizations had contact with each other
of a kind which 'expands the range of civilizations and confirms
the universal brotherhood among men.' He looked forward to the
'union and intermingling' of Indian and Western civilization once

again. In a series of essays which followed Vivekananda elaborated this idea:

India is slowly awakening through the friction with outside nations: and a result of this little awakening is the appearance, to a certain extent, of free and independent thought in modern India. On one side is modern Western science, dazzling the eyes with the brilliance of myriad suns. On the other are the hopeful and strengthening [Indian] traditions of her ancient forefathers, in the days when she was at the zenith of her glory....On one side new India is saying, 'What the western nations do is surely good, otherwise how did they become so great?' On the other side, old India is saying, 'The flash of lightening is...dazzling your eyes. Beware!' Have we not then to learn anything from the West?...Are we perfect? Is our society entirely spotless, without any flaw?....That man or society which has nothing to learn is already in the jaws of death. Yes, learn we must many things from the West: but there are fears as well. O India, the spell of imitating the West is getting such a strong hold upon you that what is good or what is bad is no longer decided by reason, judgement, discrimination, or reference to the *shastras*....O India! With this mere echoing of others, with this basic imitation of others...wouldst thou scale the highest pinnacle of civilization and greatness?[59]

This message that the blind imitation of the West as well as total rejection of the West are both equally to be eschewed, was reiterated by Vivekananda time and again. The dilemma that India of his times faced was rarely delineated as clearly as this. Needless to say there is nothing in common between Vivekananda's message urging 'learning from the West' and the British colonialist notion that India's role was that of a pupil under the tutelage of the British masters—an idea sedulously developed in British Indian historiography from James Mill onwards.[60] We should bear in mind the fact that while Vivekananda recommends discrimination in the process of 'learning from the West', he remains keenly aware of the exploitative aspect of the civilizational encounters in that age of imperialism. For instance, in the tract 'The East and the West': 'What is the message of the "progress of civilization" which the Europeans boast so much about?' That progress has meant that 'whenever the Europeans find an opportunity, they exterminate the aborigines'; the Europeans

would be very poor 'if they lived in their native homes depending
wholly on their own internal resources.'[61]

Another major theme in Vivekananda's writings is his notion
of 'unity'. There was a philosophical aspect to this notion which
is uniquely his own among nationalist ideologists. All search for
knowledge, he said, was essentially search for unity. 'Knowledge is
to find unity in the midst of diversity—to establish unity among
things which appear to us to be different from one another. That
particular relation by which man finds this sameness is called law',
for example, the laws in the natural sciences.[62] However, the notion
of unity in his writings commonly occurs in his writings in the
context of his idea of the unity of all religions. Building on the faith
of his preceptor Ramakrishna Paramahansa that all religions lead to
the same divinity, Vivekananda offers a kind of theistic universalism
as the path to India's unity. An example of the general tenor of this
approach: in the midst of vast differences in terms of race, language,
patterns of social life, and so on, 'the one common ground we have
is our sacred tradition, our religion.' Of course, any reader would
have objected that it is precisely religion which divides people
more than any other factor. But Vivekananda recognized only one
religion: 'What do I mean by one religion? Not in the sense of one
religion as held among the Christians, or the Mohammedans, or the
Buddhists.' He believed that that all religions have certain common
grounds 'however different their claims.' This was the basis of his
universalism. 'The religions of the world are not contradictory or
antagonistic. They are various phases of one eternal religion....
Therefore we must respect all religions....Religion is realization :
but mere talk...mere parroting the words of ancestors and thinking
it is religion, mere making a political something out of the truths of
religions is not religion at all.'[63] Or again consider his declaration
at the Parliament of Religions in Chicago on 19 September 1893:
Mankind, he said, needs a universal religion 'which will not be
Brahminic, Christian or Muhammedan, but the sum total of
these.'[64] Thus in Vivekananda's writings we can see a kind of theistic
universalism while Nehru's is a secular universalism, the common

ground between them being tolerance of all religions. Anyone who carefully examines Vivekananda's writings will be hard put to it find substantial evidence that he was a 'religious nationalist'.

It is well known that there was among Indian nationalists a section which equated a religious community with the nation. In thus attributing to a community nationhood, the other communities were *ipso facto* excluded. Thus their approach was exclusivist. They may be characterized as 'religious nationalists'. However, the problem is that there is an ambiguity about that word 'religious nationalism'. In the language of those who equate a religious community with a nation—for example, a 'Hindu nation' or a 'Muslim nation'— religion, as they understand it, figures prominently. But that does not mean that all those who talk of religion *and* of nationalism are therefore 'religious nationalists'. That is a fallacy which comes from confused thinking. The fallacy consists of inverting the proposition 'All religious nationalists talk of religion', to read 'All who talk of religion are religious nationalists'.

This point needs to be grasped to understand Vivekananda's approach to the idea of nationhood which was far from being exclusive. He made that clear on many occasions. It is historians who have made this issue obscure. For instance, since the Missionary historian Rev. J.N. Farquahar down to our times many historians have described Vivekananda as one of the creators of 'Religious Nationalism'. While supposedly radical historians characterize him as a Hindu nationalist, from the opposite end of the political spectrum authors like Eknath Ranade have claimed that he gave 'A Rousing Call to Hindu Nation'. Professor Hiren Mukerjee in a lecture at this Institute in 1985 said: Vivekananda 'knew, as Marx did, that men cannot make history as they please, but in building the future had to use bricks left by the past.' In his view, therefore, it is 'totally unfair to label Vivekananda's work as Religious Nationalism'.[65] A careful study of Vivekananda's writings seems to lend support to Hiren Mukerjee's views. Admittedly there are indeed some passages in Vivekananda's writings where he speaks of the need to find the common bases of Hinduism and awaken the national consciousness among Hindus.[66] But one or two such rare passages (usually occurring in Addresses to meetings of a Hindu association or local community) are insignificant compared to the vast number of the contrary kind where he emphasizes the unity of all religions.

Vivekananda spoke as a man of action. But the writings of Aurobindo (1872–1950) belong to a high intellectual plane. A first class Tripos in Cambridge perhaps made him a little unkind to persons with just average education and his fierce critique of W.G. Archer's somewhat uninformed adverse comments on Indian culture and civilization started a series of essays written by Aurobindo for the journal *Arya* in 1918–21. These essays were put together after his death under the title *The Foundations of Indian Culture*.[67] Aurobindo did not edit or publish that collection under that title; in fact, he declined to publish them unrevised and he definitely intended to 'omit all but brief references to William Archer's criticism.' That was a year before his death and he never had an opportunity to revise those essays. However, the general public came to know of Aurobindo's approach to the issue of Indian civilization from that unauthorized collection of his writings made in 1953. The original articles serialized in 1918–21 have now become available and the following discussion is based on those writings in *Arya*, his journal from Pondicherry.[68]

What were Aurobindo's main contentions on the question of Indian culture and civilization? First, he questioned the average Western critics' understanding of the civilization of India; just as an earlier generation of Indian intellectuals had pointed to the misperceptions of James Mill, Aurobindo focused upon the inadequacies of the Western commentators in his times, such as William G. Archer, or among those more sympathetic to Indian culture, Sir John Woodroffe who wrote a book with a provocative title *Is India Civilized?*[69] Aurobindo observed that quite often there was 'a feeling of recoil of the average occidental mind at its first view of the unique characteristics of Indian culture....The cultured mind tends to diminish the force of these prejudices' but the average mind fails to overcome the prejudices.[70] In the distant past there was no barrier of prejudice of this kind. Drawing upon his knowledge of Greek literature, Aurobindo says that the Greek mind, for instance in Pythagoras or the Neo-Platonists or Menander or Megasthenes, was able to appreciate much in Asiatic culture; but the modern European over-values 'rationality' and regards 'Indian religion to be an irrational animistic cult of monstrosity.' To Aurobindo the positivist rationalism inspiring Western criticism of Indian spiritual and religious thought-systems was basically an inability to recognize a different type of experience. 'There is nothing here that would warrant us in abasing ourselves before the idol of positivist reason or putting the aim of Indian culture at all lower than the spirit and aim of Western civilization....Different it is, inferior it is not....' Aurobindo believed that the Western critics' disesteem for a 'different' culture was due to the fact that in the twentieth century India was particularly disadvantaged by the historical circumstances. They are

attacking India when she is prostrate and in the dust and, materially, Indian civilization seems to have ended in a great defeat and downfall....It is an easy task in this age of the noble culture of Reason and Mammon and Science doing the works of Moloch, when the brazen idol of the great goddess of Success is worshipped as she was never before worshipped by cultured human beings.[71]

That brings us to the second major theme in Aurobindo's exposition. He elaborated on the history of Indian civilization. Aurobindo looks back upon the historical evolution in very general terms—indeed the narrative is without any reference to specific time and space, which makes it difficult either to validate or to refute that account. But nevertheless it is a powerful evocation of the spirit of the civilization.

Its first period was that of a great spiritual out flowering in which the forms were supple, flexible and freely responsive to its essential spirit. That fluid movement passed away into an age of strong intellectuality....There came as a consequence a period of richly crystallized fixity shaken by crises which were partly met by a change of ideas and a modification of forms.

But the hard binding of set forms triumphed at last and there was a decline of the inspiring spirit, a stagnation of living force....[72]

In fact Aurobindo's treatment of history is comparable to the style of the 'Philosophical Historians' who were associated with Scottish Orientalism, and unlike the more empirical tradition that dominated British Indian historiography.[73] Aurobindo refers to the period of the Vedas and the Upanishads as the first period, followed by crystallization and fixity of forms in the second period, that is, 'the later middle period of the *shastras* and the classic writings, the age of philosophy and science, legislation and political social theory and many sided critical thought, religious formation, art, sculpture, painting and architecture.' From the thirteenth century, Aurobindo observes, there began a period of decline and by the time the Western impact arrived India was 'in the supreme crisis in the life of a civilization', facing either a slow lingering death or the challenge of renewing itself through an attempt 'to understand, master and assimilate novel growths and necessities.'[74] Did this effort for self-renewal amount to a Renaissance?

Aurobindo believed that at that time, when he was writing in 1918, it was an open question whether at all there was

...really a Renaissance in India....the thing itself is only in its infancy and it is too early to say to what it may lead. The word carries us back to the turning-point of European culture....That is certainly not a type of renaissance that is at all possible in India. There is a closer resemblance to the Celtic movement in Ireland, the attempt of a reawakened national spirit to find a new impulse of self-expression which shall give the spiritual force for a great reshaping and rebuilding.[75]

Thus Aurobindo opens his series of essays on 'The Renaissance in India' in 1918. He sees at that time 'that the whole is at present a great formless chaos of complicating influences with a few luminous points of formation here and there....But it cannot be said that these forms have yet a sufficient hold on the general mind of the people.' There are interesting parallels here between the German Indological writings which have been connected with the search for national identity; it is likely that in England Aurobindo became acquainted with these writings, especially those of Schlegel, which recently Sheldon Pollock has focused on.[76] Although he believed that it was too early to judge the outcome of the process, he had developed a clear notion of what an Indian Renaissance ought to be. Though it is a long quotation it is worthwhile to reproduce his own words for it was, in a manner, a statement of his own agenda. He looked forward towards

...a process of new creation in which the spiritual power of the Indian mind remains supreme, recovers its truths, accepts whatever it finds sound or true, useful or inevitable of the modern idea and form, but so transmutes and Indianises it, so absorbs and transforms it entirely into itself that its foreign character disappears and it becomes another harmonious element in the characteristic working of the ancient goddess, the *shakti* of India, mastering and taking possession of the modern influence, no longer possessed or overcome by it.[77]

Aurobindo said that 'India can best develop herself and serve humanity by being herself and following the law of her own nature. This does not mean, as some narrowly and blindly suppose, the rejection of everything that comes to us in the stream of Time, or happens to be have been first developed or powerfully expressed by the West.'[78] This discrimination, which Vivekananda also underlined over and again, exercised Aurobindo's mind deeply. For instance, he was aware of the facile formula that only the good things which come from the West should be accepted.

I would certainly repel this formula of taking the good and leaving the bad as a crudity, one of those facile formulas which catch the superficial mind but are unsound in conception....If I accept any of these ideas it is not because they are modern or European, which is in itself no recommendation, but because they are human, because they present faithful view-points to the spirit, because they are things of the greatest importance in the future development of the life of man. [79]

If one reads Aurobindo's writings in the early stage of his days in Pondicherry, one warms to the discriminating intellect at work in his writings of this kind; it is possible that some of that intellectual quality was diluted in his works edited by others in the later years of his life as the sage of Pondicherry.

Finally, another notable feature of Aurobindo's writings on Indian civilization is his interpretation of 'spirituality'. He concedes that 'spirituality is indeed the master-key to the Indian mind; the sense of the infinite is native to it.'[80] But he qualifies this statement in many ways, unlike many other exponents of India's 'spiritual' culture. He points out that

...spirituality does not flourish on earth in the void....When we look at the past of India, what strikes us in her stupendous vitality....For three thousand years at least, indeed it is much longer—she has been creating abundantly and lavishly, republics and kingdoms and empires, philosophies and cosmogonies and sciences and creeds and arts and poems....There is no historical parallel for such an intellectual labour....Nor was all this colossal literature confined to philosophy and theology...it embraced all life, all the arts from painting to dancing, all the sixty-four accomplishments, everything then known that could be useful to life or interesting to the mind....It is when the race has lived life most richly and thought most profoundly that spirituality finds its heights and its depths....[81]

Therefore he argued that we must dismiss the idea that the tendency of metaphysical abstraction is the one note of the Indian spirit which dominates or inspires all its cadences'; it is actually 'many-faceted, many-coloured' finding expression in the application of mind to all aspects of real life. It is a spiritual tendency which 'does not shoot upward only to the abstract, the hidden and the intangible; it casts its rays down-ward and outward to embrace the multiplicities of thought and the richness of life.'[82] Thus, contrary to the tendency of many a spokesman for 'spiritual India', Aurobindo pointed out that while 'spirituality is the master-key of the Indian mind', there were other aspects to that mind, such as 'the strong intellectuality, at once austere and rich, robust and minute....Its chief impulse was that of order and arrangement' and he presumably points to the classificatory zeal with which 'all the sixty-four accomplishments' were studied, from horse-treading to dance, from politics to painting, with insatiable curiosity and 'desire to know life itself in every detail.'[83] It was the European observer who was 'struck by the general metaphysical bent of the Indian mind....by its other-worldliness', who was inclined to single out that as the only distinguishing feature of the Indian mind.[84] That was a 'one-sided' exaggeration. Thus Aurobindo distanced himself from the conventional depiction of 'spiritual India'. In his analysis of Indian art and polity he elaborated on this point.

On the whole both Vivekananda and Aurobindo were staunch defenders of traditional culture but they conceded the historical necessity of negotiating with Western civilization. They were both widely regarded as 'spiritual' leaders, but they saw the need for a notion of the 'spiritual' that was different, Vivekananda's was a neo-Vedantic activism and Aurobindo's was a totally new interpretation of man's spiritual quest. And they both had a historical vision of the greatness of India's civilization in the past and its decline in their times. They differed in their style of thinking, because Aurobindo wrote of civilization in terms of abstract analytical categories, quite unlike Vivekananda, as down to earth as one would expect of a man who travelled as a *sannyasin* to distant corners of the land. Their ability to reconcile in their distinctive manner the Western and Indian civilizations, the 'spiritual' with the materialist world outlook, accounted for their influence in twentieth century India. They prepared the Indian mind for a reappraisal of India's civilization. Perhaps that is what Nehru meant when he wrote of Vivekananda in *The Discovery of India*: 'he was a kind of bridge between the past of India and the present.'[85]

* * *

There remains a major issue with regard to the Nehruvian vision of India's civilization. There was an innate conflict of perceptions and prescriptions, a conflict between what one may call, at the cost of some necessary simplification, the 'Gandhian' and 'Nehruvian' positions. This conflict remained implicit most of the time and was not frontally faced by Nehru in his public pronouncements while Gandhi was alive. But in their correspondence one can trace it.

In the Indian discourse of civilization the idea of continuity between the past and the present sometimes generate a kind of traditionalism, a tendency to ignore that while there may be civilizational continuity, civilizations also evolve. The rhetoric in political circles about India's glorious heritage sometimes used Gandhism as a prop to defend a traditionalist position. Towards the end of 1945, with the country astir at the prospect of freedoms, the mind of the political leadership was beginning to focus on what policies India would pursue. Was the paradigm presented in *Hind Swaraj* in 1909 to be the objective?

One of the yet unexplored chapters in Nehru's life is the sharp blast of criticism he directed at the ideas of Gandhi on this issue in October and November of 1945. Nehru wrote to Gandhi:

It is many years since I read *Hind Swaraj*....But even when I read it twenty or more years ago it seemed to me completely unreal...As you know, the congress has never considered that picture, much less adopted it. You yourself have never asked it to adopt it, except for certain relatively minor aspects of it. How far it is desirable for the Congress to consider these fundamental questions, involving various philosophies of life, it is for you to judge. I would imagine that a body like the Congress should not lose itself in arguments over such matters which can only produce great confusion in people's minds resulting in inability to act in the present.[86]

He went on to say that Gandhi might have been right about '*an evil seed in civilization*' but one must not refuse to face the reality of the present and finally: 'obviously there is good, too, in the present.' Thus Nehru decisively rejected the *Hind Swaraj* and his reasons appear to be the following: First, the world was different when those ideas were propounded in 1909. 'It is 38 years since *Hind Swaraj* was written. The world has completely changed since then... In any event any consideration of these questions must keep present facts, forces and human material we have today in view, otherwise it will be divorced from reality.'[87] Second, Gandhi had unduly elevated the village as the ideal. 'I do not understand why a village should necessarily embody truth and non-violence. A village normally speaking is backward environment.' Nehru conceded to Gandhi that cities presented no admirable ideal. 'Many of the present overgrown cities have developed evils which are deplorable. Probably we have to discourage this overgrowth and at the same time encourage the village to approximate more to the culture of

the town.'[88] Third, Nehru put it to Gandhi that to attain some
minimum requirements such as 'a sufficiency of food, clothing,
housing, education, sanitation, etc.', it was 'inevitable that modern
means of transport as well as many other modern developments
must continue and be developed...If that is so, inevitably a measure
of heavy industry exists. How far will that fit in with a purely
village society?'[89] Fourth, Nehru put forward the argument that
independent India must protect itself from 'foreign aggression,
both political and economic.'[90] This requires that India develops
herself into a technically advanced country. At the same time there
is also the need to take care of keeping pace with the rest of the
world. 'In the present context of the world we cannot even advance
culturally without a strong background of scientific research in
every department.'[91]

For all these reasons Nehru was decisively opposed to the vision
of Indian civilization *Hind Swaraj* suggested more than three decades
ago. Nehru did so despite Gandhi's appeal to him: 'I have said you
are my heir. It is only proper that I should at least understand my
heir and my heir in turn should understand me. I shall then be at
peace.'[92] After an exchange of letters Gandhi and Nehru met in the
middle of November 1945 and Gandhi writes to Nehru after that
meeting: 'If in the end we find our paths are different, then so be it.
Our hearts still remain one...'[93] Gandhi appeared to believe that
in essentials there were no differences between the two. Actually
the differences remained unresolved and this became clear in the
post-independence Nehruvian policies which departed from the
Gandhian path in numerous ways.[94] Nehru, at least in letters he
wrote to Gandhi's made no secret of the fact that this is how it
was going to be, despite Gandhi's expostulations in defence of his
vision of civilization in *Hind Swaraj*. The contradiction between
the Gandhian and the Nehruvian vision of the future was not fully
examined by either of them during the exchanges between them
in 1945. And yet that was the crux of the problem of reconciling
the Gandhian outlook with the agenda of modernization. Thus
in a climactic moment in Indian history the failure to resolve that

contradiction created a dichotomy that was to characterize the
policies of the new Republic of India for decades.

NOTES

1. Jawaharlal Nehru, *The Discovery of India* (Signet Press, Calcutta,
1946; John Day, New York, 1946).
2. Nehru, 'Preface to the First Edition', *Discovery of India*, p. x.
3. Nehru, 'Epilogue', *Discovery of India*, p. 577.
4. Sarvepalli Gopal, *Jawaharlal Nehru: A Biography* (Oxford University
Press, New Delhi, 1989), pp. 148–9.
5. Jawaharlal Nehru, *Selected Works of Jawaharlal* Nehru (*SWJN*
hereafter) (Oxford University Press, New Delhi), vol. 12, p. 613.
6. *SWJN*, vol. 4, p. 322.
7. Ibid., vol. 5, p. 416.
8. Ibid., vol. 6, p. 435 (an unpublished essay found in Nehru Papers by
the editor, S. Gopal).
9. Nehru, *Discovery of India*, p. 36.
10. Ibid., p. 578.
11. Ibid., p. 49.
12. Ibid., p. 49.
13. Ibid., pp. 39–40.
14. Ibid., p. 578.
15. Ibid., p. 37.
16. Ibid, p. 77.
17. Ibid., p. 192.
18. Ibid., p. 48.
19. Ibid.
20. Ibid., p. 55.
21. *SWJN*, vol. 24, p. 204, Inaugural Address at Indian Science
Congress, Hyderabad, 2 January 1954.
22. Ibid., vol. 30, pp. 212–17, Foreword to Dinkar's *Sanskriti ke Char
Adhyay* (1955), p. 30.
23. Nehru believed that China was the only other country which could
claim three thousand years of continuity in civilizational terms. Nehru,
Discovery of India, pp. 76–7.
24. Ibid., p. 343.
25. Ibid., p. 218.
26. Ibid., pp. 219–20.
27. *SWJN*, vol. 13, p. 372.
28. Ibid., vol. 23, pp. 132–4.

29. Ibid., vol. 24, p. 181, Message to the Indian History Congress, 1953.

30. Rabindranath Tagore, 'Sirajuddaulah', a book review written in 1898, *Itihas*, (Visva-Bharati Publications, Calcutta, 1991), p. 125.

31. Notes by H.G. Stokes and H.A. Demson, 24 January 1910 Foreign Department, NAI, cited in A.R. Kulkarni (ed)., *History in Practice: Historians and Sources of Mediaeval Deccan and Marathas* (Books & Books, Delhi, 1993), pp. 138, 157.

32. Note by R.F. Schofield, 28 April 1914, Education Department, NAI, cited in Kulkarni, *History in Practice*, pp. 139, 157.

33. M.G. Ranade, *Miscellaneous Writings of the Late Mr Justice M.G. Ranade* (Manoranjan Press, Bombay, 1915), pp. 214–29.

34. This was the official view of the Revenue Department, R.D. vol. 90, 1901, p. 145, MSA, Bombay, cited in Kulkarni, *History in Practice*, pp. 132, 156.

35. M.G. Ranade, *Rise of the Maratha Power* (Bombay University, 1959, with Editorial Introduction by R.P. Patwardhan and notes by R.V. Otutker, reprint of original edition of 1900 published by Punetkar); I have preferred using this text rather than the commonly used later edition produced by the Publications Division, Government of India.

36. Lokahitavadi (1848) N.J. Kirtana (1871), V.K. Rajwade, and others had criticized Grant Duff's history earlier, but Ranade did it with greater authority than his predecessors.

37. Prachi Deshpande, *Creative Pasts: Historical Memory and Identity in Western India, 1700–1788* (Permanent Black, Delhi, 2007) pp. 80, 86.

38. Ranade, *Rise of the Maratha Power*, p. 10.

39. Ibid., p. 3.

40. Ibid., p. 4.

41. Richard P. Tucker in Kulkarni (ed.), *History in Practice*, p. 51.

42. Akshay Kumar Maitreya, *Atmakatha* (Autobiography), appended to Maitreya, *Sirajuddaulah* (De's Publishers, Calcutta, 2006; first published 1897), p. 18.

43. Akshay Kumar Maitreya, *Sirajuddaula* (in Bengali), (De's Publishers, Calcutta, 2006; first published 1897); we have drawn on his 'Autobiography', pp. 11–19.

44. Maitreya, *Sirajuddaula*, pp. 65–293.

45. Akshay Kumar Maitreya, 'The Black Hole Story', *Journal of the Calcutta Historical Society*, vol. XII, part I, no. 23, pp. 156–71.

46. Maitreya, *Sirajuddaula*, pp. 292–3.

47. Rabindranath Tagore, 'Sirajuddaula' (1898) *Itihas* , pp. 125–34.

48. Rabindranath Tagore, 'Aitihasik Chitra' (Images from History) (1899), *Itihas*, pp. 135–50.

49. Ibid.

50. See note 4 of this chapter.

51. Nehru, *The Discovery of India*, pp. 178–9, 338–43, etc.

52. Ibid., pp. 178–9.

53. Swami Vivekananda, *Complete Works of Swami Vivekananda* (henceforth *CWSV*), 9 vols (Advaita Ashrama, Calcutta, 2008), vol. VI, p. 161.

54. Vivekananda, *CWSV*, vol. IV, p. 155.

55. 'Address at Ramanad', 1897, Ibid., vol. III, p. 149.

56. Address at Manamadura, 1897, Ibid., vol. III, p. 167.

57. Vivekananda, *CWSV*, vol. V, p. 308.

58. Nehru, *Discovery of India*, p. 341.

59. 'Modern India', Vivekenanda, *Complete Works of Swami Vivekananda*, vol. IV, pp. 443, 475–7.

60. Alan Ryan, 'Introduction', in M.I. Moir, D.M. Peers, and Lynn Zastoupil (eds), *J.S. Mill's Encounter with India* (Toronto: University of Toronto Press); J. Majeed, 'James Mill's "The History of British India" and Utilitarianism as a Rhetoric of Reform', *Modern Asian Studies*, vol. 24, no. 2, 1990, pp. 209–24.

61. Swami Vivekananda, *CWSV*, vol.V, pp. 531, 535.

62. Ibid., vol.V, p. 519.

63. Ibid., vol. IV, pp. 180–2.

64. Speech at Parliament of Religions, Chicago, 18 September 1893, *CWSV*, vol. I, p. 19.

65. Hiren Mukerjee, *Vivekananda and Indian Freedom*, Calcutta, 1986.

66. For example, see *CWSV*, vol. II, p. 287.

67. Sri Aurobindo, *The Foundations of Indian Culture* (New York, 1953).

68. Sri Aurobindo, *The Renaissance in India and Other Essays on Indian Culture* (Aurobindo Ashram, Pondicherry, 1947).

69. J. Wooddroffe, *Is India Civilized* (Ganesh and Co., Madras, 1918).

70. Aurobindo, 'A Rationalistic Critic on Indian Culture', in *The Renaissance in India and other Essays on Indian Culture*, p. 103.

71. Ibid., pp. 118–9.

72. Aurobindo, 'A Rationalistic Critic on Indian Culture', in *The Renaissance in India and other Essays on Indian Culture*, p. 169

73. Jane Rendall, 'Scottish Orientalism: From Robertson to James Mill', *The Historical Journal*, vol. 25, no. 1, 1982, pp. 43–63.

74. Aurobindo, *The Renaissance in India and other Essays on Indian Culture*, p. 168.

75. Ibid., pp. 3–4.

76. Sheldon Pollock, 'Deep Orientalism?', in Carol Breckenridge and Peter Vander Veer (eds), *Orientalism and the Post Colonial Predicament*

(Philadelphia, University of Pennsylvania, 1993), pp. 76–133; Chen Tzoref-Ashkenzai, 'India and the Identity of Europe: The Case of Frederick Schlegel', *Journal of the History of Ideas*, vol. 67, no. 4, 2006, 713–34.

77. Aurobindo, *The Renaissance in India and other Essays on Indian Culture* p. 17.

78. Ibid., p. 38.

79. Aurobindo, 'Indian Culture and External Influence', March 1919, *Arya*, Sri Aurobindo, *The Renaissance in India and other Essays on Indian Culture*, p. 47.

80. Sri Aurobindo, *The Renaissance in India and other Essays on Indian Culture*, p. 6.

81. Ibid., pp. 10–1.

82. Ibid., pp. 12–3.

83. Ibid., pp. 9–10.

84. Ibid., p. 6.

85. Nehru, *Discovery of India*, p. 338.

86. J. Nehru to Gandhi, 9 October 1945, *SWJN*, vol. 14, p. 554.

87. Ibid., p. 535, (emphasis are mine).

88. Ibid.; actually thirty-six years had passed, not thirty-eight.

89. This statement of Nehru's is in response to Gandhi's in his letter to Nehru of 5 October 1945 (*Complete Works of Mahatma Gandhi* [Publications Division, New Delhi, 1999], vol. 81, p. 319) that to achieve 'real freedom ...we shall have to go and live in the villages' where 'the vision of truth and non-violence can be realised.'

90. This is one of many statements which Nehru made asserting a faith in techno-scientific progress—a point which was the subject of intense debate between Gandhi and Rabindranath Tagore; see Sabyasachi Bhattacharya (ed.), *The Mahatma and the Poet* (National Book Trust, New Delhi, 2008).

91. Nehru to Gandhi, 1945 (*CWMG*, vol. 81).

92. Gandhi to Nehru, 5 October 1945, *CWMG*, vol. 81, p. 319.

93. Gandhi to Nehru, 13 November 1945, *CWMG*, vol. 82, pp. 71–2.

94. See L.C. Jain, 'Fate of Gandhi's Economic Thinking', in Sabyasachi Bhattacharya (ed.), *Development of Modern Indian Thought and the Social Sciences* (Oxford University Press, New Delhi, 2007), pp. 19–66.

CHAPTER 5

Rethinking Indian Civilization

It is easy to pick holes in the nationalist representation of Indian civilization. Tagore or Gandhi or Nehru did not write histories for the approval of textbook committees in educational institutions. The purpose of their excursion into history was derived from an agenda different from that of professional historians. Nevertheless, if there is a mismatch between history as each of them saw it—and we have seen that there were substantial differences in their perspectives— and the history professional historians recognize, that mismatch merits our attention. Moreover, a critique of the nationalist outlook on this question is also necessary because there are issues of internal consistency—and such a consistency is, of course, a requirement in any extended argument about the interpretation of India's past. There is a third reason. Amartya Sen in a little-known lecture he gave in 1995 points to the challenges to the national perspective on the grounds favoured by 'newly empowered Hindu politics', or by those 'emphasizing the "fragments" as they are sometimes called, over the nation.'[1] Even if these challenges arise out of 'political motivations and contingencies', even if the challenges are 'ad hoc and governed by the immediacy of political agenda of particular movements', the recognition of that contingent nature of those challenges 'would not by itself, re-establish the intellectual standing of the classical nationalist interpretation.'[2]

To my mind, among the infirmities of the nationalist conception of India's civilization the most obvious one is the assumption of continuity. There are two distinct problems here. First, given the fact that there are disjunctures between cultures (for example, the Indus Valley cultures and the culture of what is commonly called the Vedic period are separated by time, by the closure of one well before the commencement of another), can we sustain a hypothesis of continuity to allow us to talk of the continuity of cultures collectively and represent them as parts of the same civilization? It is possible to imagine the succession of different cultures in different regions of the subcontinent as light bulbs dotting the map of India, each bulb coming on and going off without any necessary connection between their moments of light emission. Is not that mental map a picture nearer reality than the one we imagine in a civilization with a continuity? Is it not true that there were such complete disjunctures that in the memory of the Indian people there occurred an erasure of some of the cultures historians later placed in a neat construction of succession? The history of the re-discovery of Mauryan remains and the recovery of forgotten scripts and epigraphs of that period might provide some instances of this kind of erasure of the memory of a past culture. These are some questions which the assumption of continuity unavoidably raises.

There is a second order problem related to the continuity theory. This arises out of a conception of foundational characteristics of the Indian civilization, the notion that there is an immanent personality of this civilization, a 'unique' personality that was formed in the moment of foundation or the beginnings lost in the mist of 'times immemorial'. We have seen instantiation of this trend of thinking in earlier chapters. Today the reigning favourite concept of foundational characteristics of Indian civilization is linked with 'Vedic India'. The obvious problem here is the question, which agency is the carrier of this 'foundational' characteristic and how far back can we historically trace these characteristics?

To sum up: The 'uniqueness' of Indian civilization was frequently underlined in the Indian writings we have examined in these pages. Likewise, the continuity of Indian civilization was a recurrent theme in that literature. This continuity seems to be a chimera if one were to think of civilization as something that had for its habitation a particular territory in the subcontinent for millennia, preserved by state power with an uninterrupted history. In one part of India or another the lamp of civilization was lit and lost again over the huge span of time since the rise of the Indus Valley culture. It seems that over the long run the light travelled within the subcontinent and illuminated different regions—and thereafter those territorial entities went into darkness and oblivion so that not even folk memory preserved any residue—and long afterwards archaeologists excavated the civilization that there had flourished long ago, unremembered by the later inhabitants of that region. As a continuous territorially and politically defined entity there might have been continuity in imperial Japan or the 'middle kingdom' in China; in India civilizational continuity was a thing of a different order altogether imagined only on the assumption of a unity, spanning wide distances in space and time, and a continuity in terms of a way of life and a structure of ideas.

This perhaps is the answer to the puzzle, why the Indian writings on Indian civilization generally focus on a search for the foundational and fundamental in that civilization, for instance, the bedrock of a 'Vedic' age. The philosopher Daya Krishna has pointed out that defining the identity of a civilization involves the reconstruction of the past which includes 'the foundational images, concepts and symbols' as 'the defining point of the study of a civilization.'[3]

However, as he reminds us, while the act of understanding the civilization may involve treating the foundational as 'static and closed', a civilization which is alive in the real world is constantly subject to change; there are 'changes in the functions performed by the foundational images, concepts and symbols in which the original vision was embodied and the inevitable changes [are] introduced by the active and living use of them in the successive periods of the history of that civilization.' Given the fact that there is such change in the real world, is there any point in searching for 'something foundational in a civilization which continues to endure from the beginning to the end?' Daya Krishna's answer is in the negative. If that is accepted—and certainly most historians today would look askance at assumptions of unalterable foundational notions and consequent vision of a civilization—where does it leave us? Does it mean that there is no continuity in the identity of a civilization? Daya Krishna's answer seems to be that there is a continuity but of a different kind than that conceived in the older view of unalterable and ever-lasting constants of the foundational moment.

The continuity which persists within changes is expounded by Daya Krishna by deploying Ludwig Wittgenstein's notion of 'family resemblance'.[4] The problem addressed in that theory is: What is common between different instantiations of some supposed universal characteristic because of which a common term is applied to all the particulars under it. Why is the universal characterization applicable to members of a class when each and every member does not possess that characteristic? Wittgenstein argued that common characteristics or qualities need not be possessed by every member in order that the class name could be applied to them. His approach was to look at 'family resemblance'; it suffices if there are common characteristics between particular members x and y and between members y and z, ever in the absence of common characteristics between x and z. The originality of Daya Krishna's interpretation is to extend Wittgenstein's theory to changes over historical time. He argues that 'the theory can be applied with greater justification [that is, greater than membership of a class] to entities that change and yet possess a continuity ... According to Wittgenstein, identity over a period of time is ensured if there are common elements between stage A and B and between B and C, even if there are no common elements between A and C.'[5]

This is not merely the elaboration of a philosophical proposition. The advantage of this approach derived from Wittgenstein is that it helps us get over a common obsession when one talks of Indian civilization—an obsession with what is supposed to be foundational in that civilization, that which lasts for ever. Wittgenstein's approach enables us to see continuity within change even if one or more common characteristic is not a constant throughout history. As Daya Krishna puts it: given this approach 'we need not postulate any permanent, unchanging *atman* of a civilization, just as we need not do so in the case of a person'[6] in order to understand the continuity of personhood of a person who undergoes countless physical, psychological, and other changes during his life.

* * *

If we discard the notion of 'something foundational' to Indian civilization which continues to endure from the beginning and if we take the Wittgenstein exit from the search for universal characteristics in the continuity thesis, there remain some issues at the core of the discourse of civilization which demands our attention. Some of these issues were tangentially touched upon by Vincent A. Smith: in his introduction to the *Oxford History of India* (1919) he raised the question if it is possible to write a history of India? In other words, was there any thread of unity which ties together the discrete histories of different fragments of the subcontinent? Thus Smith came upon the answer that there was diversity but also a unity. Uninformed opinion among historians today often attributes to him the credit of conceptualizing 'unity in diversity' for the first time. This is an error and Smith probably would have disowned such credit. Far from anticipating the nationalist perspective on the syncretic unity within religious, ethnic, cultural diversities, Vincent Smith spoke only of the unity he saw in Hinduism. Second, even this unity of Hindu India despite diversities of language, environment, traditions, and so on, in the professional or academic historiography, Smith was anticipated by Radha Kamal Mookerji who wrote on *the Fundamental Unity of India* several years before Vincent Smith— and in fact Smith mentions that work.

What was Vincent Smith's notion of India's unity? Of a kind of geographical unity he had written earlier in his works on ancient India, but in 1919 in a comprehensive *Oxford History of India* from earliest times to early twentieth century, Smith raised the bigger question. Given the fact that India displayed immense diversity in terms of physical environment, ethnic composition of population, innumerable political divisions, differences in religions beliefs, and so on, how 'can a history of India be written', considering that the political unity of the country is of very recent origin. In the pre-British period 'from time to time a strong paramount power has arisen and succeeded for a few years in introducing a certain amount of political unity, but such occasions were rare.... such political union never was enjoyed by all India until the full establishment of British sovereignty....' If that was so, what makes it possible to speak of India and its history? Smith's answer was that there was unity in Hinduism. 'The most essentially fundamental Indian unity rests upon the fact that the diverse people of India have developed a peculiar type of culture or civilization utterly different from any other type in the world. That civilization may be summed up in the term Hinduism.'[7] In his opinion because of religious unity within Hinduism 'India beyond all doubt possesses a deep underlying fundamental unity....That unity transcends the innumerable diversities of blood, colour, language, dress, manners, and sect.' What of the Muslims and others? 'An Indian Muslim may be, and often is, far more in sympathy with an Arab or Persian fellow-believer than he is with a Hindu neighbour.' And Christians and others were more distant and like Muslims 'are not concerned with most of the reasons which make all Hindus one in a sense.' Even the south of India did not make it to that united entity because 'Dravidian culture' retained 'utterly un-Aryan social practices' and thus Smith believed that historians' attention must be focused on 'Indo-Aryan Brahminical culture of the north', the foreseeable future.[8]

This was Vincent Smith's idea of India's civilizational unity. The contrast between this and the nationalist discourse of a syncretic civilization is too obvious to require elaboration. Was there any affinity with the views of V.D. Savarkar? There is no affinity in terms of the political imagination that went into the making of Vincent Smith's and Savarkar's views, though both emphasize the centrality of Hinduism.

Vinayak Damodar Savarkar (1883–1966), as one would expect of him, associated the concept of civilization with Hinduism. For instance he writes about the establishment of *Hindu-pad-padshahi*: 'The very existence of the Hindus as a race, a civilization, as a faith, and as a nation, depended on the establishment of a powerful, consolidated and pan-Hindu empire.' Why was a pan-Hindu empire a necessity? It was because the Hindus, facing the Mohamedans, had 'degenerated into congeries of small states, bound together but very loosely by a sense of common civilization.'[9] V.D. Savarkar was of opinion that for the protection of 'Hindus as a race, as a civilization' it was necessary for the Marathas to establish their political supremacy, even if it involved 'using force against the Hindus themselves.'[10] On the whole in Savarkar's corpus of writings (we have chosen a historical example above) the concept of a 'Hindu civilization' recurs often, but his emphasis was on the ascription of nationhood and his interpretation of state-building under Hindu auspices. Savarkar might have written the very words which Smith wrote of the 'reasons which make all Hindus one in a sense.' But in Smith's political imagination, typical of the colonial cast of mind, that unity did not imply nationhood whereas for V.D. Savarkar such a unity was the basis of the nationhood of the Hindu community to the exclusion of others. Smith was quite emphatic that the cultural unity he saw in Hinduism was no political unity, not to speak of national unity.

Caste which, looked at broadly, unites all Hindus by differentiating them from the rest of mankind, disintegrates them by breaking them up into thousands of mutually exclusive and often hostile sections. It renders combined political or social action difficult and in many cases impossible, while it shuts off all Hindus in large measure from sympathy with the numerous non-Hindu population.[11]

Thus Smith was reassuring himself of this political ineffectiveness of the Hindu majority just eight years before the launching of the Khilafat and Non-Cooperation movement.

An old colonialist message was carried in Vincent Smith's work. The message was that political unity was attained fleetingly and in a limited way only occasionally, and it was the British who brought unity to the subcontinent. On the other hand, Radha Kumud Mookerji argued in a book entitled *The Fundamental Unity of India* published in 1914 that the 'unity generally traced to the influence of British rule in India....has really a long history, and has been an element in the historic consciousness of the Hindus from a remote age.'[12] This argument was first published in the Nationalist journal, *Dawn Society's Magazine* in 1909 and later it was elaborated to prove that 'unity is much older than British rule, that it is not a recent growth or discovery, that it has a history running back to remote antiquity.'[13] What is the evidence? (*a*) Starting from the *nadistuti* (hymn to the rivers) in *Rigveda*, Mookerji traced to Buddha's times a continuity in the concept of Bharatvarsha as a single entity. Whether indeed what was mentioned as 'Bharatvarsha' in the ancient texts he cited actually meant India as it was known in his times was open to question. (*b*) The pilgrimage prescribed and the sacred sites from Kashmir to Cape Comorin formed a deliberately created network with a view to creating a consciousness of India's unity in the mind of the Hindus. (*c*) To a lesser extent, Mookerji also drew his the evidence of the idea of political unity of India from the concepts of 'universal' sovereignty' (*chakravarti*) which one can infer from the rhetoric of ancient Kings and their adulatory memorials in texts and inscriptions. (*d*) The expansion of Indian cultural influence through the colonization of parts of south East

Asia is characterized by Mookerji as the expansion of the concept of India into a concept of 'Greater India'.[14]

The historians today have a sceptical attitude to some of these contentions. B.D. Chattopadhyaya points out some of them.

The 'Aryan-non-Aryan' binary constituents of Indian society and 'Aryanization' as the civilizing process are taken [by Mookerji] as two premises on which rests the idea of unity....Aryan-non-Aryan' dichotomy and 'Aryanization' are ideas by themselves totally inadequate for understanding the slow crystallization of the early stage of Indian civilization. Archaeology can show why [sic] for the birth of the idea of Bharatvarsha, which is identified with India, was preceded by a long series of archaeological cultures with significant spatial variations before a recognizable pattern of pan-Indian practices and symbols emerged.[15]

These archaeological evidences were not available to Mookerji in 1914.

A major characteristic of Mookerji's approach to India's civilizational unity was that he spoke of exclusively a Hindu India. This was sharply pointed out by Ramsay MacDonald (the first Labour Prime Minister of England) in his Foreword. 'What share has the Mohammedan in it? Perhaps much greater than we think.' And he went on to say 'the unity of India will not remain exclusively a Hindu conception, although its origin may be in Hindu culture.'[16] MacDonald made this point after conceding that 'many of the present governors' of India, looked upon India 'merely as a geographical expression, a mere collection of separate people, traditions and tongues existing side by side, but with no sense of nationhood in common.' Ramsay MacDonald rejected that 'Anglo-Indian' view. But he was critical of Mookerji's as well, since it excluded Muslims in India.

Notwithstanding its obvious limitations, Mookerji's thesis about the fundamental unity of India left a mark on the imagination of Indian intellectuals in the first half of the twentieth century. Despite obvious differences in their approach, one element common between the writings of Vincent Smith, Radha Kumud Mookerjee and V.D. Savarkar was the emphasis on Hinduism as the bedrock on which unity rested. The implicit (or in Savarkar's case explicit)

contradiction between this approach and the more inclusive Nationalist approach came to the forefront in the stereotype of Indian civilization as a 'Hindu civilization'. But this communalist appropriation of the civilizational discourse did not go uncontested. Not only Nehru or Tarachand, but leading spokesmen of the Muslim intelligentsia contested that exclusivist representation. The leading Nationalist Muslim spokesman Abul Kalam Azad repeatedly spoke of tolerance as the 'the great message of Indian civilization.' 'From the dawn of history Indian mind has been comprehensive, and tolerant of every kind of thought. It admitted every kind of faith and accommodated all shades of opinion....New caravans of various peoples and cultures arrived here and found their resting place.'[17] Azad went on to ask, 'shall we not prove worthy inheritors of this great heritage' of 'ancient Indian civilisation?' 'Shall we let that kind of narrow mindedness raise its ugly head which is in the air today?'[18] This was written in 1947 at a time when Nehru's *The Discovery of India* created a stir. In the rare public statements Azad made, that interpretation of Indian history remained a running theme. For instance one can see that in Azad's long preface on the history of 1857 that he commissioned Dr S.N. Sen to write in 1957.[19] Azad laid stress on 'the common life of centuries' in keeping the Hindu and Muslim communities united in the struggle of 1857. He also boldly contested sectarianism which surfaced now and then. Especially memorable was Azad's intervention in Lok Sabha when C.D. Deshmukh moved an amendment to the Bill to institute Tagore's Visva-Bharati as a central university in 1951. Deshmukh, Shyama Prasad Mookerjee, Pandit M.M. Malaviya, Professor K.T. Shah, and others wanted to insert in the statement of objectives the words 'Shantam, Shivam, Advaitam'. The Lok Sabha proceedings record the conflict between Azad as the Education Minister and these powerful members who evoked the tradition of ancient India in their support. Azad took a strong secularist position in the debate and eventually won by putting it to vote in the Lok Sabha.[20]

Azad's stance on the question of 'the message of Indian civilization' was supported in academic expositions of that theme

by leading intellectuals who shared the Nehruvian vision. Most
notable among them was M. Mujeeb, the Vice Chancellor of Jamia
Millia Islamia for twenty-five years. His *Indian Muslims* addressed
the cultural identity formed over centuries of history as well as the
issue of situating that identity in relation to India's civilizational
unity. One of his closest associates, Sayed Abid Husain authored
a book which complements Mujeeb's work. *The Destiny of
Indian Muslims* focused not so much on the history which Mujeeb
expounded, but on the contemporary predicament of Muslims in
India.[21] By and large Mujeeb and Abid Husain represent a mindset
which looked back upon a long history of two communities living
together separately and looked forward to a secular India where the
tradition of tolerance would prevail.

While the nationalist interpretation of the unity of Indian
civilization was challenged from the communalist point of view,
another challenge was posed by the north–south polarization which
became specially explicit in the early years of the Indian Republic.
One of Nehru's associates. Sardar K.M. Panikkar boldly raised the
question—in what sense and form when was the south of India part
of the Indian civilization?

A book on the same theme as *The Discovery of India* and almost
claiming equal attention in 1947 was Sardar K.M. Panikkar's
Survey of Indian History. It went through nine imprints from 1947
to 1956. This work is important for two reasons. First, he had a
considerable reputation as a historian (as an author, not merely on
account of his record of obtaining a First in Oxford) and he was also
a diplomat who was a close advisor to Prime Minister Jawaharlal
Nehru. Panikkar went beyond Nehru's more generalized treatment
of the theme of history of imperialism in Asia in writing a masterly
survey of that subject, *Asia and Western Dominance*, a work which
was soon translated into several European languages.

Second, Panikkar's writings are important because in the
discourse of civilization he brought into focus south India. His
research into the history of Kerala is not so well known, but his
Survey of Indian History—building upon research by many Indian

scholars—offered a rather original perspective on the south in relation to India. He argued that Indian civilization was incomplete until the north and the south were brought together within the ambit of a 'Hindu Civilization.'

Sardar Panikkar's *Survey of Indian History* begins with a statement of his agenda: 'text books of Indian history are generally written more from the point of view of dynasties and kings and they have but little to say about the growth of a civilization, the changes in national attitude, the development and decay of social organizations and religious beliefs and such other matters which constitute the stuff and substance of national history.'[22] Echoing Nehru, Panikkar said that their generation, brought up on books by 'foreign authors whose one object would seem to have been to prove that there was no such thing as "India"', necessitated rethinking by Indians, to 'discover India for ourselves'.[23] This critique of history-writing naturally led to an effort on the part of Panikkar to write a history of the society and culture of the Indian people.

While writing such a history Sardar Panikkar realized that when one read most of the works on early Indian history, 'one would think India south of the Vindhyas did not exist.'[24] Hence Panikkar made a special effort to integrate the histories of the north and the south. Pursuing this train of thought he argues that 'unity of India was a conscious achievement of Hinduism after the great Aryo-Dravidian synthesis had taken place.' Panikkar surmises that this synthesis began at the end of the Rigvedic age and 'this creates Indian civilization.'[25] The south remained 'different racially', although 'the composite life of Hinduism and the domination of the Sanskrit language unite both the north and the south in unbreakable bonds, proclaiming the cultural unity of India.'[26]

From our point of view today Panikkar seems to over-emphasize the role of Hinduism in uniting different parts of India. He gave a central place in his scheme of things to the Hindu scriptural prescriptions regulating secular domestic life, particularly the various rites of passage.

The *Grihya Sutra*s [a section of *Vedanga* known as *Kalpa*] determine the secular life of the Hindu householder....It is this body of domestic ritual which makes a Hindu. The dogmas of Hindus can be adopted by others.... Hindu law can apply to others....The acceptance of domestic ritual alone make a Hindu....In Indian history the most important fact, therefore, is the formulation of the discipline of the household—the *Grihya Sutras*—for it transformed the people of India who came under the influence of Hinduism into a single civilization.[27]

According to Panikkar, next in importance to the *Grihya Sutra*s were the *Dharmashastra*s. To the social regulations and rituals derived from these sources Panikkar ascribed the cementing and stabilizing element in Indian civilization: 'the maintenance of a continuous civilization through at least thirty centuries' was possible, he says, because of the regulated Hindu social organization. 'The organization of Indian civilization in its domestic and social structure, in the philosophical background which held it together, was the work of the period prior to Buddhism....The remarkable continuity of effort in the interpretation and adjustment of Dharmashastras which constitute the steel framework of this civilization is the outstanding fact of Indian history.'[28] Further, 'the history of Indian effort towards building up and maintenance of a specially Indian civilization has to be the history of the Hindu mind and its achievements.' Panikkar probably had a point to make in centralizing the Hindu belief system in his scheme of a civilization uniting the north and the south of India, but it is difficult to defend the elevation of the rituals and prescriptions and proscriptions of the Dharmashastras—which underwent from the second millennium changes to the detriment of the openness characteristic of the earlier period which allowed the confluence and commingling of various ethnic groups and cultures, as Panikkar himself recognizes. And it is curious that this compatriot of Shankaracharya should locate not him but Manu standing at the centre of the maze of Hinduism.

To examine Panikkar's position on Hinduism is not, however, our present purpose. Panikkar's original contribution was his focus on the south of India and its integration with the north as a part of the discourse of Indian civilization. His special interest in south

India showed in his other works as well. For instance, in the book on geopolitics, *Geographical Factors in Indian History*, Panikkar speculates that there is a cultural difference between the north and the south of India. 'The main differentiating characteristic is the attitude towards the sea. To the people of North India, with their central Asian traditions, the sea meant very little....The idea of ruling the seas....never entered the minds of the monarchs of the north, while it was a normal conception with the Kalingas, the Cholas, the Pandyas,'[29] Or again apropos of the differences between the north and the south, Panikkar, underlined one of the so-called lessons of history: the south must be given 'its legitimate influence in political affairs' and allowed to retain its cultural identity and 'any attempt to impose unification' by the north would 'awaken the latent feelings.'[30] which might lead to discord. The issue of regional identity within Indian civilizational unity is often explored by Panikkar—an issue which in his time linguistic reorganization of the states sought to address, not with complete success.

* * *

Given the approaches to the concept of Indian civilization we have outlined earlier, a question that arises is, how did the Marxist approach to the issue make a departure? An outstanding exponent of that theme was the Marxist historian D.D. Kosambi (1907–66). While there are anticipations of his views on Indian civilization in Kosambi's works published in 1956, 1957, and 1962, he addresses that theme systematically in the last book he produced, *The Culture and Civilization of Ancient India in Historical Outline* (1970). He begins that work with the assertion of 'the continuity that we find in India over the last three thousand years or more.'[31] What is his explanation of the continuity of Indian culture which 'is perhaps its most important feature'? He finds that continuity is the evolution of 'the material foundation of Indian culture and civilization.' He points to the succession of different stages of the evolution of the technology and organization of productions and production relations leading to the political economy of mid-twentieth century

India. On the one hand Kosambi saw in this progression of social formations a continuity, on the other hand he also saw a continuity in the survival of tools, technologies and organization of production of primitive times right through history. For instance: 'The bullock cart and village huts seen in Bharhut Sculptures of about 150 BC, or the plough and ploughman is Kushana reliefs of AD 200 would cause no comment of they appeared suddenly in some modern Indian village.'[32] Or again: 'Modern India produced an outstanding figure of world literature in Tagore. Within easy reach of Tagore's final residence may be found Santals and other illiterate primitive people still unaware of Tagore's existence. Some of them are hardly out of the food-gathering stage.'[33] In fact Kosambi made this coexistence of different modes of production and survival of pre-existing material artefacts and social relationships the basis of his method of reconstructing the past. Thus Kosambi focuses upon continuity in the material basis of Indian civilization and culture which he perceived, in line with ethnographers' definition, as 'essential ways of life of the whole people.'[34]

We have seen in the earlier pages that from R.G. Bhandarkar's times the absorption of various 'foreign' ethnic groups into the Indian population was a major theme, and that in Tagore and Gandhi's works there developed a concept of a syncretic civilization in India. Kosambi strongly endorses that notion too. The very first sentence of his book on the civilization of ancient India: 'A dispassionate observer who looks at India with detachment and penetration would be struck by two contradictory features: diversity and unity at the same time.'[35] In modern India, Kosambi goes on to say, 'in spite of this apparent diversity, there is a double unity.'[36] There is unity brought about by the 'ruling class', the modern Indian bourgeoisie, and also by the state which 'seems to stand above all classes' but serves the interests of the ruling class quite well. In ancient India, Kosambi points to the methodological possibility of reading caste stratification to explain Indian history. He observes that different cultural traditions including those of people who were assigned low caste status or kept outside the pale as 'tribals' gradually secured

...assimilation to other parallel traditions. Another step above, they have been rewritten by Brahmins to suit themselves, and to give the Brahmin caste predominance in the priesthood....Still higher we come to what is called 'Hindu' culture....The main work of brahminism has been to gather the myths together, to display them as unified cycle of stories, and to set them in a better-developed social framework. Either many originally different gods and cultures are identified (syncretism), or several duties made into a family, or into a royal court of gods. At the very top came the philosophical developments formulated by the great religious leaders of Indian history.[37]

Kosambi concludes his discussion of this process of incorporation and reordering of 'gods' of various origins, with this evaluation of the unification process: 'Brahminism thus gave some unity to what would have been social fragments without a common bond. The process was of crucial importance in the history of India, first developing the country from tribe to society, and then holding it back, bogged down in the filthy swamp of superstition.'[38] He particularly paid attention to the incorporation of tribal groups into the 'general agrarian society', sometimes eventually into the caste system, and the admission of their gods into a system Brahmins propagated; it was a 'mechanism of acculturation, a clear give and take', which allowed 'Indian society to be formed out of many diverse and even discordant elements.'[39]

The fact that Kosambi endorsed the notions of the continuity and the unity of Indian civilization does not mean that he accepted the nationalist perspective in entirety. In his review of Nehru's *The Discovery of India* in 1946, published in the Marxist theoretical journal *Science and Society*, Kosambi was highly critical. He said that he was an 'admirer of the author' but he could see in the book shortcomings due to the difficulty the author had in jail in accessing books and sources. The important point he made was that the Nehruvian perspective failed to attempt a class analysis in understanding Indian history.[40] Unlike many nationalist thinkers' pecans of praise for India's culture and civilization, Kosambi heavily underlined the wretched condition of the subordinated classes in India. 'The modern Indian village gives an unspeakable impression of grimmest poverty and helplessness....The surplus taken away from people who like in such misery and degradation nevertheless provided material foundation for Indian culture and civilization.'[41] Kosambi believed that the Indian class structure merited special attention because it had certain specificities which marked it out from the journalese picture commentary in use.[42] He had expanded this view in 1951 in the *Monthly Review* but later he added to that the formulation that 'Caste is class on a primitive level of production.'[43]

Finally another difference between Kosambi's approach to the Indian civilization and that of the nationalists was that he does not seem to look upon the stability of India's civilization as something to applaud. What is stability to one man may be stagnation to another. Kosambi contends that stability was secured at the cost of subjection to a regime of superstitions and primitiveness, especially in rural India. In this regard he follows Marx's tendency of thought; at one point he even quotes Marx on 'the idiocy' of rural existence. He really let himself go on Brahminism as an element in ancient India culture:

The logic advanced by the *Brahmins* took good care to avoid all reality.... [An] ability to swallow logical contradictions wholesale also left its stamp upon the Indian national character, noticed by many observers as by Arabs and Greeks before them. The absence of logic, contempt for mundane reality, the inability to work at manual tasks, emphasis upon learning basic formulas by rote with the secret meaning to be expounded by a high guru, and respect for tradition (no matter how silly) backed by fictitious ancient authority had a devastating effect upon Indian science.[44]

This delightful denunciation—which reminds us of Tagore's later writings—is, of course, about India's culture in total decline, 'some fifteen centuries after Asoka.' Thus stagnation was the end product of what was once a stability that had integrated and advanced society. This is how Kosambi presents the dialectics of stability and advancement, on the one hand, and unity and diversity on the other.

D.D. Kosambi was a polymath who made original contributions in diverse areas including pure mathematics, quantitative numismatics, Sanskrit studies, and ancient Indian history. But he is remembered today chiefly for his work as a historian. That is not without reason. That is where he made an enduring impact even if some details of his findings and observations may be open to question in the light of later research. If we try to evaluate his contribution to the interpretation of history the most enduring and wide-ranging in significance appears to be his approach to the idea of India as a civilization. In posing wide-ranging questions about the civilization in India Kosambi differed from the general run of academic historians of his times for they rarely engaged in the discourse of civilizations. In engaging with that discourse Kosambi was swimming against the current. The specialized and fragmented view in the academic historians' professional writings did not usually add up to that vision of totality which the notion of civilization demands. The fact that Kosambi was never given his due by them in his lifetime can be, arguably, ascribed to their disdain for a non-professional who was not only an avowed Marxist, but also given to talking about a dubious entity called 'civilization'.

That raises finally another question. What explanatory weight is to be assigned to Kosambi's Marxian method in our effort to understand and contextualize his approach to the civilizational discourse? In a humorous letter to his old friend Daniel Ingalls, Indologist at Harvard, he wrote in 1953: 'The world is divided into three groups: (1) swearing by Marxism, (2) swearing at Marxism, (3) indifferent, i.e. just swearing....I belong to (1), you and your colleagues to (2).' Perhaps Kosambi's adherence to Marxism was to its use as a method, not as a source on par with empirical sources of knowledge. He allowed that in some respects there was a poor fit between Indian history and the classical Marxian scheme. But he consistently used Marx's method as a tool. And hence his scorn for 'theological' tendencies in Marxism. In his Introduction to *Exasperating Essays*, he writes: 'Indian Official Marxists hereafter called OM' were often displeased with him but he could not but protest their 'theological emphasis on the inviolable sanctity of the current party line, or irrelevant quotations from the classics.' In using Marxist method in his own lights, in his effort to construe the history of civilization in India, in the convergences and divergences between his approach and the nationalist discourse of civilization, D.D. Kosambi has left much for us to try and understand and evaluate.[45]

***

The discourse of civilization is usually on diachronic lines, but the sociologists' and anthropologists' attempts to understand civilization is not historical, it is synchronic. While historians in the mid-twentieth century were exploring the bases and the limits of India's civilizational unity, G.S. Ghurye or N.K. Bose addressed a similar set of questions from the synchronic angle. Primarily this was the sociologists' response to the nationalist discourse of civilization. In part their concern with the theme of civilization stemmed from the debate among contemporary anthropologists such as A.L. Kroeber, Robert Redfield, Milton Singer and others.

G.S. Ghurye (1893–1983) had a long tenure as professor of sociology in Bombay University (1924–59), having succeeded the first professor of sociology, Sir Patrick Geddes. Ghurye made the comparative study of ancient civilization and culture a required course of study at the graduate level in his department since he believed that it was a desideratum for studying sociology. At least three of his works were specifically on that subject, *Culture and Society* (1947), *Occidental Civilization* (1949), *Cities and Civilization* (1962). Ghurye's approach was from the angle of historical sociology and he had the advantage of Indological training in his early days. He drew upon his knowledge of Sanskrit texts and ancient history. Nirmal Kumar Bose (1901–1972) was not only an ethnographer but also an activist in the Nationalist movement. He was in the Non-Cooperation movement in 1921 and in 1946–7 he was secretary to Mahatma Gandhi and wrote a moving account of that experience. His first publication in 1929, a study of the Indian spring festival, drew the attention of the eminent anthropologist A.L. Kroeber who reviewed it very favourably. One can see some common elements between Bose's line of work and that of Ghurye. We shall examine the views of Bose who displayed a more pronounced nationalist proclivity in his writings. Bose insisted, in a manner unusual among social scientists of his generation, the need for autonomous development of Indian anthropology, the need to liberate it from dependence on Western exemplars and teachings. 'The position of Indian Anthropology has, on the whole, been colonial in relation to schools which have dominated the European or American scene from time to time.'[46]

When Bose was the Director General of the Anthropological Survey of India he radically departed from the conventional lines of research in that institution, a hide-bound bureaucratic creation of the British times. One of his objectives was to develop a research agenda of conducting synchronic studies to demarcate diverse culture zones and to identify common elements which unify India. It was, so to speak, an attempt to explore through anthropological data the basis of India's unity. He initiated a vast project to study material culture traits in 430 villages in 311 districts and the outcome was a report entitled *Peasant Life in India: A Study of Indian Unity and Diversity.*[47] The subtitle of his report spells out his agenda. Bose was of the view that 'there is more differentiation at the material base of life and progressively less as one moves higher and higher.'[48] There is some originality in the way he mapped diversity and unity. He put forward what has been called his 'pyramid theory': as one goes to the top the structure tapers to a point where there is much greater ideological unity while there is more diversity in the lower steps—a diversity which is knit into a kind of emotional unity through the mechanism of culture communication by means of oral tradition.

Bose gave due weight to the factor of ethnic diversity but— here he switches from the synchronic to the diachronic mode of thought—'the country has harboured in her spacious bosom, from prehistoric times, various races and cultures, both immigrant and autochthonous from the Old Stone Age cultures to those of Austric, Dravidian, Aryan and Mongoloid.'[49] And yet, he contended, there was a trend towards the merger of the fragments into the greater whole. In a paper curiously entitled 'The Hindu Method of Tribal Absorption' (1941) he developed the notion of the 'tribe-caste' continuum in India.[50] This notion formed the basis of a widely used paradigm of absorption of tribal groups into the mainstream of Hindu peasant society and the caste system. Like Kosambi, Bose considered caste a major factor in unifying Indian society, though it was otherwise considered an abomination.

An important part of Bose's approach to civilizational unity was that he postulated a continuous dialogue between the local and the sub-continental in Indian civilization towards developing a 'confederation of cultures.'[51] Bose published his early formulations on this in 1929.[52] There are many elements in common between Bose's ideas in this regard and the set of ideas encapsulated in the terms 'Great Tradition' and 'Little Tradition' introduced by a school of anthropology in North America led by A.L. Kroeber and Robert Redfield.[53] While their notion of civilization resembles Bose's approach to the Indian civilization, they theorized in a more systematic way than Bose who tended to give to theory less attention than he did to his empirical data.

We have noticed in previous chapters some Indian intellectuals' perception of the integration of various cultures into the fabric of Indian civilization. It was now possible to bring such empirical observations within the domain of a theory of cultural integration. Although the work of A.L. Kroeber (1876–1960) and Robert Redfield (1897–1958) was originally in a different empirical context, the concepts of the Great Tradition and Little Tradition helped Indian sociologists to explicate the dialogue between the local and the regional cultures on the one hand, and the larger entity, the Indian civilization, on the other. Kroeber in his widely used book *Anthropology* (1948) argued that some cultures or categories of cultures are more particularly civilizations. In his writings, especially the posthumously published *Styles and Civilizations* and *An Anthropologist Looks at History,* he advanced the argument further through analysis of writings on cultures by Spengler, Toynbee, and Sorokin.[54] Robert Redfield pushed forward towards positing a continuous dialogue between on the one hand 'Folk Society' and 'Civilization', the 'primitive cultures' and the more advanced and complex cultures characterized by urbanization, writing, higher level of reflective and creative 'works of the mind'.[55]

It is best to read Redfield's subtle treatment of the issue in his own words. 'The *unity* of a civilization is, I suggest, its identity as defined by its substantial qualities. A civilization, like other cultures, may be thought of not as a congeries of perfectly homogeneous elements, but rather as having a oneness from attributes that refer to very much or all of it.' These attributes are

...a characterizing set of kinds of social relationships, or perhaps a persisting, prevailing set of views as to the nature of what is and ought to be....[The] historian who is farthest from the scientists' disposition to abstract and generalize, gives his kind of unity to a civilization by choosing from out of all that happened...certain events, and not others, and by relating some of those events to others.[56]

Redfield also suggested that each civilization has a form 'that remains the same when everything else changes...[thus] a civilization may be thought of as having a form that remains the same while the content, the institutions, messages, beliefs, change.' He offers the term 'form' as a synonym for the commonly used terms 'pattern' 'structure', 'style'. He emphasized the fact that a civilization is thought of not only in terms of social structure but also styles of thinking and doing things, or patterns of values and ideas. He says that it is natural to study 'synchronic forms' in primitive societies, since little is known of their past. 'Civilized peoples, as in the studies of national character, may also be so conceived [that is, synchronically]. But a civilization, as something not the same as a civilized people, seems strongly to connote its long history' and thus one is naturally drawn to the diachronic mode of studying a civilization.[57]

Robert Redfield's definition of civilization as 'formed things of the mind', evidently belonging to the domain of Great Tradition, and the contraposition of the Little Tradition of the locality or region was a crucially important intervention which influenced anthropological and sociological studies of the generations after N.K. Bose, for example, the research of Surajit Chandra Sinha, Bernard S. Cohn, MacKim Marriott and others. As Redfield saw it, these observers emphasized the existence of 'networks' and 'centres', that is, 'a concentration of civilizational influence.'[58] Sinha for instance underlines, within the larger entity Indian civilization, interactions between the tribal, peasant and feudal state in pre-colonial India.[59] Bernard S. Cohn and MacKim Marriott's study of the 'networks and centres in the integration of Indian civilization' was on lines analogous to Redfield's approach.[60] MacKim Marriott studied rural 'little communities in an indigenous civilization.'[61] Milton Singer studied 'the Great Tradition in a metropolitan centre', Madras city.[62] M.N. Srinivas's concept of 'sanskritization' did not belong to this family but its adoption was eminently possible.[63]

Thus there developed an altogether new approach to the civilization in India from the perspective of social anthropology. Robert Redfield outlined that approach in retrospect in 1958:

A civilization is an interaction of many little local cultures and a 'high culture', 'great tradition', that is considered, developed and eventually written down by thinkers and teachers provided with the time to create works of the mind and connected with religious or philosophical institutions....A civilization is...a compound culture; rural people and townspeople are apart, different and traditionally inter-connected....Peasants are dependent in important part on the moral and ideational authority of intellectual elites characteristically resident outside of the villages, in towns, shrine-centres, temples or monasteries.[64]

Thus the local or peasant community is heteronomous, that is, dependent on norms coming from without, since 'civilizations developed their Brahmins, Mandarins, or Imams to expound, for the whole civilization, *dharma*, the Confucian ethnic, or *dar-ul-Islam*.' Hence one sees

...a large overarching conception of a civilization as an arrangement for communication between components that are universal, reflective, and indoctrinating, and components which are local, unreflective and accepting ....The real structure of tradition, in any civilization or part thereof, is an immensely intricate system of relationships between the levels and components of tradition, which we enormously oversimplify by referring to as 'high' and 'low', or as 'great' and 'little'.[65]

An important consequence of the approach thus outlined by Redfield was that the historical orientation of Indian anthropologists like G.S. Ghurye and N.K. Bose received a positive endorsement from the dominant Western practitioners in the discipline. In place of an exclusively synchronic study, there came into the field a diachronic approach as well in the research book of many anthropologists. Redfield observed that synchronic study was adequate for a 'look at the surviving civilizations that we may directly experience in China, India, Islam or "the West"' but it was not adequate when we look at the intellectual production and emotional attachments formed over centuries and playing a vital role as source of the 'high tradition'.[66] There was no getting away from history if one wanted comprehensively to understand any civilization. Thus space was created for a new ethno-historical approach to Indian cultures and civilization.

The conceptual framework developed by Kroeber, Redfield, and Singer deeply influenced research in cultural anthropology and in particular the social history of the absorption of tribal groups into the mainstream of Hindu peasant society and the caste system. Perhaps a problem here was the valourization of the hegemonic Great Tradition. Although Redfield's original formulation was a fairly nuanced depiction of a complex relationship, it was open to the criticism that it presented an artificial contraposition. A contemporary of Kroeber, the art historian Ananda Kentish Coomaraswamy (1877–1947) presented a different notion altogether. In his writings on the arts and crafts of his own country Ceylon and India, and in the series of essays which were collected under the title *Dance of Siva*, Coomaraswamy depicted Indian civilization as a community

where the masses and the elite shared a common aesthetic sensibil-
ity. He saw no differentiation between bearers of a Great Tradition who handed down to denizens of Little Tradition aesthetic
standards and creations. According to him 'Hindu and Buddhist
civilizations' displayed a 'feudal and theocratic culture' where 'the
countryman and the courtier' shared in common a 'hieratic art'
which was a 'communal' or the popular heritage of the entire society. Hence there was no distinction between high art for the elite
and craft for the masses.[67] The significance of Ananda Coomaraswamy's observations, beyond the domain of art history, is that he
represents a point of view which rejects the contraposition between
high and low culture. When Kroeber and Redfield developed later
the concept of Great and Little Tradition, such a contraposition was
indeed made, perhaps because anthropology had not yet worked
out a way out of the dichotomy, 'primitive' and 'civilized'.

* * *

While the historicity of civilizations attracted attention in sociology
and anthropology in the middle decades of the twentieth century, it
is curious that among professional historians in India the substantial
literature on world civilizations—the works of Arnold Toynbee,
Oswald Spengler, Pitrim A. Sorokin, and others—had little or no
impact. Nor did it influence the way Indian intellectuals imagined
their civilization. Jawaharlal Nehru is the only notable author
who refers to these works, especially Spengler. Academic authors
eschewed reference to them perhaps because of a strong British
tradition of empiricism from the late nineteenth century. Or again,
a factor might have been the social organization of knowledge
production: avoidance of the larger discourse of civilizations on a
global scale was natural in the pursuit of research degrees by careful
cultivation of a minute area of research 'given' by a supervisor
who had worked under similar conditions in an Indian or British
University. Above all the intellectual tradition in the universities
was such that except for a Kosambi or a Panikkar, the average

academic felt uncomfortable with somewhat abstract categories such as 'civilization'.

And yet, there was a great deal in these comparative global studies which endorsed the views expounded in the nationalist historical discourse in India. For instance, Oswald Spengler (1880–1936). While the early nineteenth century European perspective, reflected in James Mill's evaluation of India's civilization, was premised on a faith in the enduring superiority of European civilization, exactly opposite was the perception of Spengler. Almost exactly a hundred years after James Mill, Europe's prospect as Oswald Spengler saw it was encapsulated in the title of his work, *The Decline of the West* (1918). Subject to the cyclical trajectory of civilizations waxing and waning, Europe too was headed for a decline. Beyond this doomsday declaration, Spengler had another objective. In his book, he said, 'narrowly there is an analysis of decline of that West European culture which is now spread over the entire globe. Yet the object in view is the development of a philosophy and the operative method of comparative morphology in world history.'[68] Thus his work was intended to be not only an empirical but also a methodological contribution towards developing history of civilizations.

Spengler also writes of the bias in Western perception which Indian nationalists harped upon. The 'Western thinker', Spengler said, lacked 'insight into the historically relative character of his data', he lacked awareness of his 'duty of looking beyond them to find out what the men of other cultures have with equal certainly evolved for themselves.'[69] It has often been said that Spengler's work anticipates the emergence of Nazism in Germany. Be that as it may, it certainly needs to be noted that some of his ideas bore a strong resemblance to those of a section of Indian Nationalists.

While the prophet Spengler was scarcely heard in India, the historian Arnold Toynbee (1889–1975) was fairly widely known in India, even though he acquired no following among historians. His favourable reception was partly because his style of exposition was free of the Germanic abstractions of Spengler, and partly because he was a prominent man in the intellectual circles of England with whom many Indian intellectuals desired affiliation. However, the range of his scholarly work on the twenty-one major civilizations he identified deterred imitation of his comparative studies on a global scale. Like Spengler's work, Toynbee's ten stout volumes produced between 1934 and 1954 showed clearly how far the perspective from the West had shifted since James Mill and his generation. A *Study of History*[70] reflected the changes the world saw in the position of England and West European Powers in the inter-War period, the World War II and its aftermath. Perhaps the most remarkable thing about Tonybee's view of the world was the recognition of a plurality of civilizational trajectories of development. That view replaces the early nineteenth century European notion of a linear pattern in all human history progressing, or failing to progress, towards the civilization of Western Europe as it was in early nineteenth century. This recognition of plurality was his most significant contribution along with his argument that as an 'intelligible field of study' civilization is the most appropriate and irreplaceable. The profusion of empirical data in his *Study of History* and his tendency to refrain from highlighting his theoretical propositions concealed from the common view the theoretical infrastructure of his exposition. In India there was not enough appreciation of the field he opened up, the comparative study of civilizations. As we have noted earlier, civilization as a category was not part of the professional historians' bag of tools in the world of Indian academics.

Nevertheless the discourse of civilization entered through the backdoor with the help of the burgeoning literature on nationalism from the 1980s, in particular the works of Ernest Gellner (1983), Benedict Anderson (1983) and Eric Hobsbawm (1992).[71] With the restoration of nationalism to a central place in political studies, a mass of empirical historical research which came in a rush in the post-independence decades found a theoretical anchorage. Re-thinking on nationalism naturally brought into focus the issue of historicity of nations and this led to greater awareness of the relevance of 'civilizations', that is, the continuity and unity of a cultural kind over a long period of history. As Anthony D. Smith has observed, there was 'a centrality of the debate about the antiquity of nations' due to the 'vital role that historical sequence and periodization play in explanations of the constituent process of nation formation.' Almost all the historians of nation formation 'have taken the question of the nation's genealogy and historicity as their starting-point and axis of explanation engaging, implicitly or explicitly, in a debate "when is the nation?"'[72]

Anthony Smith has provided in his study of *The Antiquity of Nations* (2004) a survey of the variety of approaches to the issue of a nation's historicity, with a focus on the long run, the period prior to the emergence of modern nationalism. The problem in Smith's approach seems to be that he neglects the utility of the notion of 'civilization' when he points to a simplicist dichotomy between 'the modernist' and 'the perennialist' answer to that question. In his view the 'modernists' are those who consider nations as 'recent and novel' and nationalism as 'the product of modernization'.[73] As distinct from them, the 'perennialists' are those who find a 'persistence of nations or ethnic communities...and their ability to endure over the *longue duree*'; this is possible due to 'the enduring roles of myths and symbols which guard the community against outsiders and their cultures', and 'cultural factors of religion, language, myth, custom, art and historical memory'.[74] Smith questions the 'myth of the modern nation', underlines the importance of the 'ancient—that is the rooted, original, and persistent elements', to 'establish the antiquity of nations in both a historical and sociological science. Historically, it opens up the question of pre-modern nations....'[75] A rather dubious extension of the term 'nation' is necessitated by this theoretical position; it is not clear why the existence of *civilizational* unity in the pre-modern period prior to the evolution of nationalism in the modern period is not considered by Smith as a more appropriate framework.

One outcome of the publication of works like Anthony Smith's or John Armstrong's *Nations before Nationalism* on medieval Europe and West Asia, was the production of Indian historians' research on analogous lines.[76] Apropos of Benedict Anderson's 'imagined community', Smith remarked, 'Why only imagined? Why not also, even primarily for most people, "felt"?'[77] Rajat Kanta Ray's book on *The Felt Community* is a laudable attempt to prove the existence of patriotic bonds in India prior to the emergence of modern nationalism in India under British rule.[78] The problem is that due to the multiplicity of languages, in India sources for this kind of research are accessed by any individual only through translation; pre-selected sources alone are available in translation, adequate familiarity with the nuances of language and specificities of regions are difficult to acquire, and thus the project cannot advance much beyond the print culture, modern education, response to English ideas, etc. Perhaps that is why C.A. Bayly anticipated Ray's line of argument by several years but did not push the argument beyond a critique of the view that national or patriotic sentiment in India was solely a product of British rule, and an outline of an argument in respect of the eighteenth and nineteenth century for which sources in the English language are copious.[79]

The assertion of the pre-British origins of a sense of Indianness, whatever may be the category one may employ to describe that, is important because the idea that India was a British invention is not altogether dead. As late as 1997 a historian as perspicacious, as Sunil Khilani writes: 'What made possible the self-invention of a national community was the fact of alien conquest and colonial subjection....After all, before the nineteenth century, no residents of the subcontinent would have identified themselves as Indian.'[80] At the same time, Khilani qualifies what he says when he adds that 'it is too simple to see India as pure invention', and points to the common cultural forms, mythic narratives, aesthetic and ritual motifs, caste, etc., which were the bases of a coherence. Now, surely that is what civilizational unity is about. This proposition as we have seen in these pages, was advanced by Indian nationalists a century ago. The nationalist contention was that India was not a British invention—unless one were to accept their definition of it in terms of territoriality, administrative structure, and European traits of nationhood. This contention rested on a notion of civilizational unity.

Finally, we must consider, in the context we are in, a very influential work which accords a central place to the category 'Civilization'—Samuel P. Huntington's *Clash of Civilizations*.[81] The article in *Foreign Affairs* which preceded the book publication carried a modest question mark after the title. But the book title dropped the question mark and in response to a good deal of criticism, Huntington, in another article in the same journal, claimed that he had proposed a paradigm shift. He cited Thomas Kuhn and claimed that the paradigm of clash between civilizations was superior to any other for contemporary global politics.[82] He argued that

As with any paradigm, there is much that *the civilization paradigm* does not account for....Yet, as Kuhn demonstrates; anomalous events do not falsify a paradigm. A paradigm is disproved only by the creation of an alternative paradigm that accounts for more crucial facts in equally simple or simpler terms....The debates the civilizational paradigm has generated around the world show that in some measure, it strikes home....

Huntington's also claimed that events in international politics could be predicted from his paradigm.

It is possible to argue that Huntington's work is irrelevant to the theme of this book, whatever may be the merit of his paradigm in the study of global politics. Nevertheless it is necessary to take note of his work since Huntington's 'civilization paradigm' is so influential that in many academic circles you mention the word 'civilization' and you raise an expectation that you would talk about Huntington's work. The work is irrelevant not only because it is chronologically irrelevant in our present context. There are other deeper-seated reasons. To begin with, Huntington's work is not about 'civilizations' at all, it is about power blocs which have changed since the end of the Cold War era. The fact that some of these power blocs consist of countries which have some common cultural features, often derived from religious belief systems, does not necessarily make them civilizational categories. In Part One of his book, Huntington divides the world into eight 'major civilizations'.

These are Sinic, Japanese, Hindu, Islamic, Orthodox (Christian), Western, Latin American, and African. This classification is peculiar in that the *differentia specifica*, separating one unit from another, are not self-consistently employed. Of these so-called civilizations in Huntington's scheme two are geographically defined (Africa, Latin America), three are defined in cultural terms (Sinic, Japanese, Western civilizations), and three are defined solely in terms of the dominant religion (Hindu, Islamic, Orthodox Christian). Not only does this classificatory scheme defy all logic of classification, but it also fails to meet the test of utility in empirical terms. What kind of civilizational unity does Africa possess and does it possess even the semblance of political unity? In the 'remaking of world order' what role has been played by Hinduism to justify the classification of India in religious terms? Perhaps the same question is valid for Orthodox Christianity. Further, Huntington's approach to the 'Islamic civilizations' is an ideal example of what Edward Said characterized as Orientalist essentialization.

Huntington's thesis also suffers from lack of internal consistency. He argues that with modern technology there is increasing cross-cultural communication and thus similarities among cultures steadily increases; at the same time, he also asserts that the notion of a single culture is a thing of the past. He is right in saying that modernization is not Westernization, but the cultural attributes of modernity remain unexplained. And if, as he argues in part two of his book, increasing importance is accorded to religion, how is that to be reconciled with that modernity? In Part Four of the book when we come to the core of the issue, clashes between civilizations, Huntington hazards a historical narrative of the past conflicts between Islam and Christianity, but when it comes to modern times there is a silent elision from 'Christianity' to 'the West' as the adversary of Islam. That unavoidable elision suggests that all the stuff about Crusades and conflictual relations in the past are rather irrelevant since the adversaries are not the same, and the *casus belli* are also vastly different. Huntington describes how Islamic fundamentalists denounced their adversaries in the First Gulf War as 'Crusaders'. Such rhetorical flourishes scarcely helps him to prove continuity between medieval Islam's conflicts with Christian powers and the conflict between a few West Asian countries and the modern Western powers—as proposed by Huntington. As we hurtle through history in the company of Huntington, towards his defining paradigm, one develops a doubt whether the 'simple map' of global politics in the past and now is a bit too simple. Even if one were to accept such a map to serve the limited purpose of somehow arriving through history to the 1990s, there remain conceptual problems. How correct is it to dress up as 'civilizations', entire continents like Africa, regional alliances between states, people in various social and political formations sharing nothing except a religions mania, and Sinic or Indic or European civilizations? These are some of the reasons why it will be inappropriate to take Huntington's work on clash of civilizations as relevant to the discourse of civilization.

* * *

The theme of civilization has been brought into the historians' agenda in recent times by diverse routes. First, the search for identity formed prior to nationhood, the 'antiquity of nations', has been one route, as we have seen. Second, the enormous literature spawned by the debate on Orientalism since Edward Said has also led to civilizational issues.

It will be neither necessary nor possible to launch into a discussion of the ever-growing literature on Orientalism. But it may be useful to look at the some aspects of it relevant to our present concerns. It is obvious that Edward Said's Foucauldian approach to Orientalist knowledge as a discourse of power is very important in that it accorded recognition to the complicity of the Orientalists' knowledge-enterprise with the European consolidation of hegemony in the East. Such a sense might have been a sub-text of a good deal of nationalist writings criticizing nineteenth century European attitudes to Indian civilization. However, Said's was a vastly more explicit, a theoretically informed, and academically well-founded critique which swept almost all before it. That simultaneous

onslaught on Euro-centrism in scholarship on the one hand, and
its colonialist political affiliation on the others, raised heckles, but
it also could be seen as a long-awaited answer from civilizations
which suffered grievous misrepresentation in colonialist hands.

It is interesting in hindsight, to see that the few 'native'
intellectuals Edward Said cited were from the ranks of 'progressive
nationalists' like K.M. Panikkar in India or Anwar Abdel Malek
in Egypt. When Said quotes statements on the Orientalized orient
'perfectly characterized by Anwar Abdel Malek', or the Occident–
Orient relationship in K.M. Panikkar's 'classic' *Asia and Western
Dominance*, Said is drawing upon the nationalist critique of
colonialism.[83] And Said explains his own engagement with the
theme of Orientalism in terms of his personal awareness of

...being an 'Oriental' as a child growing up in two British colonies.
[Palestine and Egypt]....In many ways my study of Orientalism has been
an attempt to inventory the traces upon me, the Oriental subject, of the
culture whose domination has been so powerful a factor in the life of all
Orientals....The nexus of knowledge and power creating 'the Oriental' and
in a sense obliterating him as a human being is therefore not for me an
exclusively academic matter.[84]

Needless to say, Edward Said's thesis on Orientalism developed
an argument that went way beyond that of the nationalist intellectuals, but the cast of mind created by those intellectuals was
certainly an influential factor in the favourable reception of Said's
thesis in Asian countries.

The problem with Said's historical analysis is that the essentialism which he detected in Orientalism crept into his own characterization of Orientalism. That characterization is essentialist in the
sense that he totalized in his narrative the whole of the Orientalist
endeavour, regardless of variations in time and space. It was the kind
of essentialism that Gandhi and other nationalists deployed in their
strategy in respect of the 'West' (see Chapter 2 of this book). At the
same time, it must be conceded that when detailed historicization is
made by Said, the scholar in him did perceive distinctions between

various phases and aspects of Orientalism. He points out those distinctions in respect of India. He surmises that to many Orientalists in the beginning of the nineteenth century the Orient was the 'Orient of the *Sakuntala*, the Zend Avesta, and the Upanishads.... [T]he "good" Orient was invariably a classical period somewhere in a long-gone India, whereas the "bad" Orient lingered in present-day Asia, parts of North Africa and Islam everywhere.'[85] And likewise he draws attention to another kind of Orientalism which influenced the manner in which Europe envisioned India, an Orientalism which Said finds, for instance, in Karl Marx. According to him Marx ultimately takes his stand 'in the protective Orientalized Orient', Marx's ideas about the 'regenerative' role of British rule in India is a piece of 'pure romantic Orientalism' envisioning Europe 'regenerating a fundamentally lifeless Asia', and Marx's India was part of an Orientalist 'collective abstraction'.[86] It is true that there are shades of Orientalism in Marx's rhetoric, all that about 'Hanuman the monkey god', and so on, particularly in the popular history he sketched in the newspaper the *New York Daily Tribune* which Said quotes leaving out much else Marx wrote on India. At the same time, Said is less than just in overlooking the fact that Marx's was a critique of precisely that hegemonic power which was the site of the creation of the Orientalists' approach to Indian civilization. Said does of course, recognize 'Marx's humanity, his sympathy for the misery of people.' But Said seems to look upon Marx's approach to the Indian question as an exercise in constructing an abstraction, derived from Orientalist thinking, in order to provide an 'illustration of a theory'. There is in Marx, Said concedes, a humanist sympathy, but that 'wash of sentiment...disappeared as it encountered the unshakable definitions built up by Orientalist science'; therefore ultimately the human sympathy is replaced by an 'Orientalist vision'. It is true, again, that Marx is 'fitting into' his theory the Indian situation; but a superficial resemblance between his view of the stage of India and the Orientalist view seems scarcely adequate to condemn his views as ultimately of Orientalist lineage.

In fact a profound problem lies here: How far can one push the enterprise of tracing lineage of ideas through parallelism between one set of texts and another?

However, while there are debatable points such as these, the achievement of Said's outstanding work was to bring back into the agenda of historians the great theme of civilization. The impact that has had in the area of Indian studies has been debated by, among others, Gyan Prakash, Rosalind O'Hanlon, and David Washbrook.[87]

A question which has cropped up in recent research into Orientalism is the status of the 'dialogue', 'exchange', 'interaction' between the early Oriental scholars and their native informants, the pandits and the maulavis. This is relevant to our theme. The point to ponder is whether the recently 'discovered' process of, 'exchange' between European Orientalists and their native pandit informants is a process which forms a part of the process we focus on in this book, Indians 'talking back'. Just as there was at one time a good deal of interest in the complicity of the native 'elite' in running the British Indian Engine, there has developed a line of research in recent times purportedly foregrounding the role of the native informants in Orientalist construction of Indian literature and history. This line of research bifurcates to produce two kinds of map of the situation. On the one hand we have historical accounts which underline the continuity of native knowledge systems and knowledge institutions, for example, Christopher Bayly makes that unexceptionable point in his work on *Empire and Information* (1996) and elsewhere.[88] That is a useful corrective to the 'blank slate' fallacy. The second position other scholars arrived at, starting from the same point, is a somewhat different narrative of 'dialogue', 'exchange', etc. between the imperial authorities or knowledge producers, and the pandits and other native informants. Thus, for instance, Philip Wagoner has presented the pandits as independent agents and not merely as passive collaborators, Eugene Ircshick emphasizes the complicity of natives in production of new knowledge or of new significations, while Homi Bhabha began a trend which underlined the negotia-tions between native and colonial participants in producing 'hybrid'

culture (as opposed to the earlier tendency to highlight the uni-
lateral and external imposition of the Western knowledge system
and culture).[89]

Even after we make an allowance for the fact that these approaches are more complex and nuanced than the earlier depiction
of Orientalists without the least acknowledgement of the existence
of native informants and colleagues, there is no doubt that these
ideas of 'exchange' or 'dialogue' do not give due weight to the
asymmetries in the relationship between the native subjects and the
colonial masters in the productions of colonial knowledge. Michael
Dodson, a Sanskrit scholar with pioneering scholarly work on the
Banares College and James Ballantyne, the Principal from 1846 to
1861, is right when he observes: 'In intellectual histories of colonial
India (or rather histories of knowledge), we might...ask whether
the attempts made to emphasise the complexity of epistemological processes in the form of "dialogue" or "exchange" have been
sufficient to invoke the kind of historical complexities in imperial
relationships which seem desirable without inherently sacrificing
the broader picture of empire as inimical.'[90]

The fact of the matter is that the social context of knowledge
production is crucial. The 'exchange' between the pandits and
European Orientalists in the early nineteenth century took place
in a context of abject dependence of the pandits on their European
patrons. The context was quite different when Bankimchandra
or Tagore were responding to the European discourse on Indian
civilization; the general state of subjection of India to British rule did
not immediately impinge on the Indian participants' autonomy in
so far as their intellectual production was concerned. Undoubtedly
they remained a subjected people within the empire, but they were
also true agents in the intellectual domain, that is why they could
talk back to Europe.

* * *

There are some methodological issues which we kept in abeyance
till now in this book, since experience shows that quite often

those who talk of methodology in the beginning have eventually nothing substantive to say. We have seen that some of the colonial historians—some, not all of them—constructed a history of a civilization in India which was at a low stage of development, and it was a civilization which was arrested at a stage of development which was far behind that of Europe in the eighteenth century. James Mill was the most prominent exemplar of this trend of thinking and his political message was loud and clear: Utilitarian ethic demands that the British should play their appropriate role in history as the masters of a subject race stagnating at a low rung in the ladder of civilization. From an adversarial point of view there developed in the nationalist discourse another tradition of interpreting history, to contest the disparaging representation of Indian civilization in the hands of colonial historians. India began to talk back. But in the course of the twentieth century that conversation went beyond the limited need to satisfy hurt pride or to stoke resentments. When we describe that discourse as 'nationalist', we aggregate diverse approach to the notion of the Indian civilization. As we have seen, there were many differences, explicit or implicit, among the various exponents. The self-reflexive exercise of deliberating on issues of methodology was rarely undertaken. Some of those questions which relate to the narrative presented in the preceding chapters need to be addressed now.

In his work *Culture and Society: 1780–1950*, Raymond Williams, after having traced the trajectory of evolution of many words like 'democracy', 'industry', and 'class', concludes that the word 'culture' 'with all its complexity of ideas and reference' is the most crucial among all those concepts. 'For what I see in the history of this word, in its structure of meanings, is a wide and general movement in thought and feeling', comprehending the totality of changes in respect of society and common life.[91] The term 'civilization' in the Indian nationalist discourse as well as colonial writings, plays a comprehensive and multi-dimensional role similar to that of the term 'culture'. This has been our contention in this book. His method of inquiry was to concentrate on 'particular thinkers and their actual statements'; thus 'the framework of the inquiry is general, but the method, in detail, is the study of individual statements.'[92] In retrospect our method in this book was not unlike Raymond Williams', but unlike the scene surveyed by Raymond Williams, in India one encounters a much larger panorama and many more participants in the discourse of nationhood and civilization. That difference in scale gives rise to the question, are we creating an unreal construct when we talk of a 'nationalist discourse' of India in the singular?

The question is whether it will be correct to speak of 'the nationalist discourse', given the fact that there were substantial differences in outlook within the nationalist school. In the earlier chapters we have pointed to these differences. At the same time, we have aggregated the whole as the nationalist discourse. Perhaps it is possible, without essentializing a thing that was diverse in form, to adopt an epistemological position which has been implicitly taken by many historians of ideas. That position may be stated as follows: in its *divulgent* form nationalism is heterogeneous and changeful, but there is an *immanent* form of that ideology which has a unity and continuity through changes and diverseness. No doubt 'nationalism' is an ideology which has changed over time, responding to objective situations its proponents encountered, and to the subjective proclivities of those proponents. But beyond those changes and diversities, is there not an inherent and more enduring set of elements in that ideology? If so, that is what allows us to posit the category 'nationalist discourse'. The use of these categories does not necessarily deny the fact that its constitutive elements are historically contingent categories and they refer to things which change over time, and synchronically vary over space.

Edward Said in his study of *Orientalism* provides a useful description of his methodological approach:

My principal methodological devices for studying authority here are what can be called *strategic location*, which is a way of describing the author's position in a text with regard to the Oriental material he writes about, and *strategic formation*, which is a way of analyzing the relationship between texts and the way in which groups of texts, even types of texts, even textual genres, acquire mass, density, and referential power among themselves and thereafter in the culture at large.[93]

This is a fairly accurate description of the method generally followed by historians of ideas, and the present work on the idea of civilization in nationalist writings is no exception.

Another issue that needs to be addressed from the methodological point of view is as follows. There seems to be an assumption, perhaps an affectation among those anxious to be politically correct, that to engage in the discussion of 'Indian civilization', is tantamount to entering into complicity with the mythologization of India's past towards conservative or reactionary ends, including a communalist construction of India's past. An analogous complicity is assumed in engagement with the discourse of nationalism and an illogical slide enables the identification of 'nation' with the 'nation state'. Needless to say the approach in the historical imagination we have studied in this book, rejects both these tendencies of thought.[94]

One possible defence of denying the validity of history of civilizations is, of course, the denial of all totalizing narratives—a part of post-modernist critique of historiography. Ashis Nandy, for instance, finds much to recommend in the 'anti-historical stance of post-modernism.' He draws attention to the link between the idea of history and the modern nation state and surmises that the historical worldview exported from the West to the non-Western world has 'helped rigidify civilizational, cultural and national boundaries.'[95] According to him older civilizations like India were ahistorical, but in recent times historical consciousness 'owns the globe' and 'the politically powerful now live in and with history.'[96] There remain some societies in the periphery which still live in a state of ahistoricity and they have myths to organize the experiences of the past. Nandy argues a case for ahistoricity 'on grounds of diversity, seen as a moral value in itself, especially when it is located in the worldview of the victims.'[97] Thus stated as a moral choice Nandy's position leaves no room for argument; you can contest that position only by stating a different moral choice. There are reasons, which

Nandy prefers not to enumerate, to sympathize with his position. But what does one make of the allied line of reasoning driven by the idea that for the entire 'non-Western' world the only totalizing narrative is that of the nation state?

The best philosophical exposition on those lines is perhaps in Dipesh Chakrabarty's *Provincializing Europe* (2001).[98] 'Why is history a compulsory part of education of the modern person in all countries today, including those that did quite comfortably without it until as late as the eighteenth century....It does not take much imagination to see that the reason for this lies in what European imperialism and third-world nationalism have achieved together: the universalisation of the nation state as the most desirable form of political community.'[99] He concedes 'the capacity of Indians to act as subjects', that is, to assume agencyhood, and that they have a sense of history which 'we in the universities' would recognize. Then he goes on to say that Indian history

...speaks from within a meta narrative that celebrates the nation state; and of this meta narrative the theoretical subject can only be a hyper real 'Europe'....The mode of self-representation that the Indian can adopt here is what Homi Bhabha has justly called 'mimetic'. Indian history, even in the most dedicated sociologist or nationalist hands, remains mimicry of a certain modern subject of European history and is bound to represent a sad figure of lack and failure.[100]

There is no doubt that a notable feature of knowledge production at the global level is what Chakrabarty has aptly characterized as 'the subalternity of non-Western history.'[101] Nor is there any doubt that 'Europe works as a silent referent in historical knowledge' and that 'Third-World historians feel a need to refer to works in European history, historians of Europe do not feel any need to reciprocate.'[102] Whether this asymmetry is a result of 'cultural cringe...on our part, or cultural arrogance on the part of European historians', is of little consequence except when one is personally exposed to such experience in certain countries. But the important point Chakrabarty makes is the representation of India as a case of failure to adequately mimic the European model. The familiar argument about the master narrative, centralizing the nation state, leaves no space for considering the attempts to construct an alternative narrative in civilizational terms, the attempt we have tried to focus upon in these pages. Perhaps this is because an acknowledgement of its existence would seriously hamper the representation of the metanarrative of the nation state as the only mode. It might have been perhaps useful for him to consider whether the mimetic moments, in real life or in representations, coexisted with an alternative approach where the category 'civilization' figured much more than the putative nation state.

In this context it is necessary to bear in mind the fact that what has been characterized above as history as 'we in the universities' regard it, has been redefined by many historians in recent times. A common point made in the European writings of the nineteenth century on Indian civilization was the absence of historical works and a sense of the historical. James Mill, as we have seen in the first chapter of this book, wrote a good deal about this absence. In recent years many historians of India have argued for the existence of historical literature in the Indian tradition and thus they have questioned the European attribution of absence of historical consciousness in India. When James Mill in his history of India asserted that there was no indigenous tradition of writing history he took for granted that the European style of historicizing the past was the only mode of recording the past. It is now being suggested that modes different from the one current in Europe were used in pre-modern India. This argument has many variants. Romila Thapar[103] points to the *itihasa-purana* tradition and demonstrates how it is possible to recover 'real' history from out of the tradition in which it is embedded. On the other hand David Shulman and Sanjay Subrahmanyam can see in pre-modern indigenous writings not only sources from which history can be recovered, but also a genre of writings which are in themselves works of history. They show instances of 'powerful forms and modes of writing history' in south India from the sixteenth to the eighteenth century in Telugu, Tamil, Sanskrit, Marathi, and Persian texts according to folkepics, courtly poetry or *kavya*, and prose narratives.[104] Nicholas Dirks has coined a neologism, ethno-history, but he tends to look upon the indigenous narratives relating to the princely state he has studied more as a special kind of source, not quite as works of history.[105] Anthony K. Warder on the other hand recognizes in a whole range of texts recording memories of the past a genre which merits classification as works of history.[106] Ashis Nandy endorses India's first psychoanalyst Girindra Sekhar Bose's approach to 'the techniques that the epics-as-*histories* followed'.[107]

Without multiplying examples of claims to historical status, the outcome of this trend can be summed up as a tendency in recent historiography to admit of and look for alternatives to the 'Western' notion of what history is and ought to be. This cast of mind has been most clearly expressed by Shulman, Subrahmanyam and Rao: they intend to

refute the notion that history was an 'alien' import brought in, for better or for worse, by colonial rule....In Western Europe, history did emerge as a relatively fixed and stable genre, even before the positivist turn of the nineteenth century....Each community writes history in the mode that is dominant in its literary practice. By the same token, newly ascendant or powerful cultures may deny history to the communities they seek to dominate, and historicity to their texts. What constitutes history is not a given, in some universal sense, but practices specific to time and place.[108]

They firmly reject the post-modernist attempt to obfuscate the distinction between history and other forms of literature and demonstrate how there exist a series of Indian historiographical texts and how sensitivity to the 'texture' help in identifying historical narratives. While their objective was to show that history and historical consciousness did exist in the time and space they studied, south India from sixteenth to eighteenth century, the more general point that emerges is the need to recognize the plurality of genres and modes of history-writing.

Finally we come to the question, how objective was the nationalist evaluation of the civilization in India? Needless to say, the very fact that we are looking at the *nationalist* approach means that there was a particular tilt in their narrative and interpretation;

but they made a claim, as we have seen, to correct from an objective
point of view the colonialist bias in the representation of Indian
civilization and history. We have to bear in mind the fact that
in the late nineteenth century and the early half of the twentieth
the positivist notion of objectivity, associated with historians like
Leopold von Ranke (1795–1886) was dominant. We have noted
that the more perceptive of the nationalist intellectuals, Nehru for
instance, acknowledged that their view of history was qualified by
the nationalist perspective and Nehru made no bones about it. It is
interesting to note in Amartya Sen's analysis of the epistemological
question of 'positional objectivity' one sees a philosophical defence
of objectivity of a qualified kind.[109] Sen's stance in this regard
is probably important for other reasons as well in the over-all
development of his philosophical position; the kernel of this
argument appeared in essays presented in Yale in 1990, in University
of Kansas in 1992, in a paper published in the journal *Philosophy
and Public Affairs* in 1993, and in his recent work *The Idea of
Justice* (2009).[110] Sen makes a distinction between objectivity in
terms of 'uncompromisingly universalist terms (what Thomas Nagel
has called the view from nowhere)' and objectivity in the 'positional
perspective, as the view from a specified delineated somewhere.'[111]
The positional perspective is not a subjective point of view because
it comprehends 'actual observations and the objective interpretation
of those observations'; however, 'the nature of the observations and
the conclusion drawn are inescapably influenced by the position of
observation.' Sen exemplifies his point that positional observation
cannot be dismissed as subjective in this manner: the sun looks
about the size of the moon from the view point of an observer on
the earth, but that is not a subjective observation, it is a positional
observation. We need not reproduce all of Sen's argument here
but the essential point that emerges is that rather than stick to a
standard of absolute objectivity, or 'the view from nowhere', it will
be useful to move away from such epistemology and metaphysics
to 'practical reason', and to 'assess the different views in terms of
their respective implications for action and to evaluate them in that

light.'[112] Thus we invoke 'practical reason, in addition to epistemic concerns', in order to deal with the 'view from somewhere', that is, positionally qualified observations which we actually get in real life.

Sen brings his epistemological position into an interface with the problem of historical interpretation.

The interpretation of history and of culture are peculiarly mediated by the positional features of observation and interpretation. Each individual thing about the past that is observed can be understood in a particular way depending on the nature of the questions that engage and motivate the inquiry....To dismiss the positional variabilities as mere 'subjectivism' would miss out something substantial in the nature of objectivity (not all objectivity is about 'the view from nowhere'—some relate to a specified 'somewhere') and it would miss the fundamentally impersonal quality of positional views....[113]

What Sen calls 'positional observation' is impersonal in the sense that it can be checked and confirmed by different persons from similar positional situation, and is shared at an interpersonal level. Amartya Sen's intervention is important for at least two reasons. First, it recognizes observation of things in the past as historically contingent, breaking away from unreal demands of objectivity in absolute and universalist terms. Second, he deploys practical reason as opposed to pure knowledge: Anticipating his later work on identity in India, he writes in 1996: 'The problem of our identities also involves both epistemology and practical reason....We are not settling issues of pure knowledge only....'[114]

These are some of the methodological considerations which qualify the narrative offered in the previous chapters of this book. While looking back at the nationalist discourse of civilization we have to bear in mind the need to avoid some common errors of interpretation in histories of ideas. It will be necessary to guard against the tendency of mind to hypostatize the idea of civilization into an entity. A reified idea thus acquires a life of its own. It will be equally necessary to heed Quentin Skinner's warning against what he calls 'the mythology of prolepsis', and consistently ask whether the retrospective meanings attributed in interpretation are the same as what the authors of cited texts meant.[115] Above all it will be useful to guard against the temptation to make the story too neat. However, one may perhaps concede that one can indeed see, as they say in film-land, a strong 'story-line' when one looks at India talking back.

NOTES

1. Amartya Sen, *On Interpreting India's Past* (Asiatic Society, Calcutta, 1996), p. 22; this is the text of Sen's lecture at the Asiatic Society, 20 March 1995.

2. Ibid., pp. 2–3.

3. Daya Krishna, *Prologomena to Any Future Historiography of Cultures and Civilizations* (Project of History of Indian Science, Philosophy and Culture [PHISPC] and Munshiram Manoharlal, Delhi, 2005), pp. 44–7.

4. Daya Krishna draws upon Ludwig Wittgenstein, *Philosophical Investigations* (trans. G.E.M. Anscombe, New York, Macmillans, 1973).

5. Krishna, *Prologomena to Any Future Historiography of Cultures and Civilizations*, pp. 82–5.

6. Ibid., p. 83.

7. Vincent Smith, *Oxford History of India* (Oxford university Press, Oxford, 1919), p. 10.

8. 'Introduction', ibid., pp. viii–xi.

9. V.D. Savarkar, *Hindu-pad-padshahi or a Review of the Hindu Empire of Marathas* (Pune, 1925), reprint in V. Grover, *Political Thinkers of Modern India* (Deep and Deep Publications, Delhi, 1992), vol. 14, p. 131.

10. Ibid., p. 141.

11. Smith, *Oxford History of India*, Introduction, p. 10.

12. Radha Kumud Mookerji, *The Fundamental Unity of India* (Bharatiya Vidya Bhavan and Chronicle Books, 2003; first published in London, 1914), p. 32.

13. Ibid.

14. Ibid., pp. 48–79.

15. B.D. Chattopadhyay, 'A Historical Note', in *The Fundamental Unity of India*, pp. 140–1.

16. J. Ramsay MacDonald, 'Introduction to the First Edition', in *The Fundamental Unity of India*, pp. 17–20.

17. Abul Kalam Azad, 'Convocation Address', Patna University, 21 December 1947, (ed.) *Selected Works of Abul Kalam Azad* (ed.) Ravindra Kumar (New Delhi, 1991), vol. III, pp. 105–6.

18. Ibid., p. 106.

19. Surendra Nath Sen, *Eighteen Fifty-seven* (New Delhi, 1957).

20. Azad, *Selected Works of Abul Kalam Azad*, vol. V, Document nos 39–43, Progs. of House of the People, 28 April 1951, 30 April 1951, 1 May 1951, 2 May 1951, 3 May 1951.

21. M. Mujeeb, *Indian Muslims* (London, 1962); S. Abid Hussain, *The Destiny of Indian Muslims* (Har Anand, Delhi, 1965, 1993).

22. K.M. Panikkar, *A Survey of Indian History* (Asia Publication, Bombay, 1954, 1st edition, 1947) p. VI.

23. Ibid., p. VIII.

24. Ibid., p. 3.

25. Ibid., p. X.

26. Ibid., p. X.

27. Ibid., p. 237.

28. Ibid., p. 238.

29. K.M. Panikkar, *Geographical Factors in Indian History* (Bharatiya Vidya Bhawan, Bombay, 1959) pp. 78–9.

30. Ibid., p. 110–1.

31. D.D. Kosambi, *The Culture and Civilization of Ancient India in Historical Outline* (Vikas Publishing House, Delhi, 1970; first edn Routledge, London, 1965), p. 9. The seeds of Kosambi's thoughts on Indian civilization are to be seen in *Introduction to the Study of Indian History* (Popular Prakashan, Bombay, 1956); *Exasperating Essays: Exercises in Dialectical Method* (Popular Book House, Poona, 1957, reprint India Book Exchange, Calcutta, 1977); *Myth and Reality* (Popular Prakashan, Bombay, 1962).

32. Ibid., p. 16.

33. Ibid., p. 2.

34. Ibid., p. 10.

35. Ibid., p. 1.

36. Ibid., pp. 2–3.

37. Ibid., pp. 15–16.

38. Ibid., p. 22.

39. Ibid., pp. 170, 172.

40. Reprint of review in Kosambi, *Exasperating Essays*.

41. Ibid., p. 17.

42. Kosambi, *Exasperating Essays*.

43. Kosambi, *The Culture and Civilization of Ancient India*, p. 50.

44. Ibid., pp. 174–5.

45. Kosambi, *Exasperating Essays*, p. 5.

46. N.K. Bose, *Fifty Years of Science in India: Progress of Anthropology and Archaeology* (Indian Science Congress, Calcutta, 1963), p. 1.

47. N.K. Bose (ed.), *Peasant Life in India: A Study of Indian Unity and Diversity* (Anthropological Survey of India, Calcutta, 1961).

48. 'Introduction', ibid.

49. N.K. Bose, 'The Geographical Background of Indian Cultural Heritage', 1937, cited in N.K. Bahera and K.K. Mohanti, 'Bose on the Unity of Indian Society and Culture', in R.K. Bhattacharya and J. Sarkar (eds), *Passage Through Indian Civilization* (Anthropological Survey of India, Calcutta, 2002), p. 199.

50. N.K. Bose, 'The Hindu Method of Tribal Absorptions', *Science and Culture*, 8 October 1941, lecture at Indian Science Congress.

51. Bahera and Mohanti, 'Bose on the Unity of Indian Society and Culture', p. 204.

52. Bose, *Cultural Anthropology* (Arya Sahitya Bhavan, Calcutta, 1929, reprints 1953, 1963); Bose, 'Contact of Cultures', *Calcutta Review*, vol. 54, nos 1–3, 1935; 'Hindu Social Organization', *Visva-Bharati Quarterly*, new series, vol. I, no. 4, 1936.

53. Robert Redfield, 'The Folk Society', *American Journal of Sociology*, vol. 52, no. 4, January 1947, pp. 293–308; A.L. Kroeber, *An Anthropologist Looks at History* (Berkeley, University of California Press, 1963).

54. Kroeber, *An Anthropologist looks at History*; *Styles and Civilizations* (Greenwood Press, West Port, CT, 1973).

55. Redfield, 'The Folk Society'.

56. Robert Redfield, 'Civilizations as Things Thought About', in *Human Nature and the Study of Society: The Papers Robert Redfield* (ed.) Margaret Park Redfield (Chicago, Chicago University Press, 1962), vol. I, p. 373.

57. Ibid., p. 375.

58. Ibid., p. 384.

59. Surajit C. Sinha, 'Tribal Cultures of Peninsular India as a Dimension of the Little Tradition', in Milton Singer (ed.), *Traditional India: Structure and Change* (American Folklore Society, Philadelphia, 1959).

60. Mackim Marriott and Bernard S. Cohn, 'Networks and Centres in Integration of Indian Civilization', *Journal of Social Research*, Ranchi, vol. I, no. 1, 1958, pp. 1–9.

61. McKim Marriott, 'Little Communities in an Indigenous Civilization', in McKim Marriott (ed.), *Village India* (University of Chicago, 1955).

62. Milton Singer, 'The Great Tradition in a Metropolitan Centre: Madras', in Singer (ed.), *Traditional India*.

63. M.N. Srinivas, *Religion and Society among the Coorgs of India* (Clarendon Press, Oxford, 1952).

64. Redfield, *Human Nature and the Study of Society*, p. 404.

65. Ibid., pp. 393–5.

66. Ibid., p. 404.

67. Ananda Kentish Coomaraswamy, *Arts and Crafts of India and Ceylon* (T.N. Foulis, London, 1913); *Dance of Siva: Fourteen Indian Essays* (Asia Publishing House, Bombay, 1952; first edn 1918); *What is a Civilization and Other Essays* (Oxford University Press, New York, 1989).

68. Oswald Spengler, *The Decline of the West* (English translation) (Knopf, New York, 1926, reprint, Oxford University Press, New York, 1991), chapter I, section III, p. 5.

69. Oswald Spengler, *The Decline of the West*, pp. 10–11, 39–40.

70. Arnold J. Toynbee, *A Study of History*, 12 vols (Oxford University Press, Oxford, 1934–61).

71. Ernest Gellner, *Nations and Nationalism* (Blackwell, Oxford, 1983); Benedict Anderson, *Imagined Communities: Reflections on the Origin and Spread of Nationalism* (Verso, London, 1983; second edition 1991); Eric Hobsbawm, *Nations and Nationalism since 1780* (Cambridge University Press, Cambridge, 1990).

72. Anthony D. Smith, *The Antiquity of Nations* (Polity, Cambridge, UK, 2004), pp. 3–4.

73. Ibid., p. 14.

74. Ibid., pp. 9–10.

75. Ibid., pp. 25–6.

76. John Armstrong, *Nations before Nationalism* (University of North Carolina Press, Chapel Hill, 1982).

77. Anthony Smith, *The Antiquity of Nations*, p. 99.

78. Rajat Kanta Ray, *The Felt Community: Commonality and Mentality before the Emergence of Indian Nationalism* (Oxford University Press, New Delhi, 2003).

79. C.A. Bayly, *Origins of Nationality in South Asia: Patriotism and Ethical Government in the Making of Modern India* (Oxford University Press, New Delhi, 1999).

80. Sunil Khilani, *The Idea of India* (Hamish Hamilton, London, 1997), pp. 154–5.

81. Samuel P. Huntington, *The Clash of Civilizations and the Remaking of World Order* (Simon and Schuster, New York, 1996).

82. Samuel P. Huntington, 'The Clash of Civilizations', *Foreign Affairs*, no. 72, 1992–3; and 'If Not Civilizations, What?', no. 73, November–December, 1993.

83. Edward Said, *Orientalism* (Pantheon, London, 1978), pp. 5, 96.

84. Ibid., pp. 24–6.

85. Ibid., pp. 98–9.

86. Ibid., pp. 153–5.

87. Gyan Prakash, 'Orientalism Now', *History and Theory*, vol. 34, no. 3, 1995, pp. 199–212; Gyan Prakash, 'Writing Post-Orientalist Histories of the Third World', *Comparative Studies in Society and*

History, vol. 32, no. 2, 1990, pp. 383–408; Rosalind O'Hanlon and David Washbrook, 'After Orientalism: Culture, Criticism and Politics in the Third World', *Comparative Studies in Society and History*, vol. 34, no. 1, 1992, pp. 141–84.

88. C.A. Bayly, *Empire and Information* (Cambridge University Press, Cambridge, 1996).

89. P.B. Wagoner, 'Pre-colonial Intellectuals and the Production of Colonial Knowledge', *Comparative Studies in Society and History*, vol. 45, no. 4, 2003, pp. 783–814; Eugene F. Irschick, *Dialogue and History: Constructing South India, 1795–1895* (University of California Press, Berkeley, 1994); Homi Bhabha, *The Location of Culture* (Routledge, London, 1994); Bhabha (ed.), *Nation and Narration* (Routledge, London, 1990).

90. Michael S. Dodson, *Orientalism, Empire, and National Culture: India 1770–1880* (Cambridge University Press, Cambridge, and Foundations, Delhi, 2009), p. 12.

91. Raymond Williams, *Culture and Society, 1780–1950* (Chatto and Windus, London, 1958, reprint 1982), pp. 17–18.

92. Ibid., p. 18.

93. Said, *Orientalism*, p. 20.

94. Many of the proponents of these ideas make no more than imitative noises. For instance, in a country which never experienced the Enlightenment, to proclaim that Enlightenment is a 'Bad Thing' is an absurd imitation of the critique of Enlightenment in Europe. Likewise, without some knowledge of what was the concept of civilization in the nationalist writings, to attempt its critique is somewhat odd.

95. Ashis Nandy, 'History's Forgotten Doubles', *History and Theory*, vol. 34, no. 2, May 1995, pp. 44, 49.

96. Ibid., p. 46.

97. Ibid., p. 47.

98. Dipesh Chakrabarty, *Provincializing Europe: Post-Colonial Thought and Historical Difference* (Oxford University Press, New Delhi, 2001).

99. Ibid., p. 41.

100. Ibid., p. 40.

101. Ibid., p. 42.

102. Ibid., p. 28.

103. Romila Thapar, *Interpreting Early India* (Oxford University Press, New Delhi, 1992); *Time as a Metaphor of History: Early India* (Oxford University Press, New Delhi, 1996).

104. Velcheru Narayana Rao, David Shulman, and Sanjay Subrahmanyam, *Textures of Time: Writing History in South India, 1600–1800* (Permanent Black, Delhi, 2001), p. 23.

Bibliography

Anderson, Benedict, *Imagined Communities: Reflections on the Origin and Spread of Nationalism* (Verso, London, 1983, second edition 1991).

Armstrong, John, *Nations before Nationalism* (University of North Carolina Press, Chapel Hill, 1982).

Azad, Abul Kalam, *Selected Works of Abul Kalam Azad* (ed.) Ravindra Kumar (New Delhi, 1991).

Bahera, N.K. and K.K. Mohanti, 'Bose on the Unity of Indian Society and Culture', in R.K. Bhattacharya and J. Sarkar (eds), *Passage Through Indian Civilization* (Anthropological Survey of India, Calcutta, 2002).

Ballantyne, T., *Orientalism and Race: Aryanism in the British Empire* (Palgrave, Basingstoke, 2002).

Bayly, Christopher, *Empire and Information* (Cambridge University Press, Cambridge, 1996).

———, *Origins of Nationality in South Asia: Patriotism and Ethical Government in the Making of Modern India* (Oxford University Press, New Delhi, 1999).

Bhabha, Homi, *The Location of Culture* (Routledge, London, 1994).

———, (ed.), *Nation and Narration* (Routledge, London, 1990).

Bhandarkar, R.G., *Collected works of Sir R.G. Bhandarkar* (ed.) V.G. Paranjape and N.R. Utgikar, 4 vols (Bhandarkar Oriental Research Institute, Pune, 1928–33).

105. Nicholas B. Dirks, *The Hollow Crown: Ethno-history of an Indian Kingdom* (Cambridge University, New York, 1987).

106. Anthony K. Warder, *Introduction to Indian Historiography* (Popular Prakashan, Bombay, 1972); also see his *Indian Kavya Literature*, 7 vols (Motilal Banarasidass, Delhi, 1971–2004).

107. Nandy, 'History's Forgotten Doubles', pp. 44–66.

108. Rao, Shulman, and Subrahmanyam, *Textures of Time*, pp. 3–5.

109. Amartya Sen, *On Interpreting India's Past* (Asiatic Society, Calcutta, 1996), pp. 4–9.

110. Amartya Sen, *The Idea of Justice* (Allen Lane, London, 2009), chapter 7.

111. Sen refers here to Thomas Nagel, *The View From Nowhere* (Clarendon Press, Oxford, 1986).

112. Sen, *The Idea of Justice*, p. 7.

113. Ibid., p. 6.

114. Ibid., p. 9.

115. Quentin Skinner, 'Meaning and Understanding in the History of Ideas', *History and Theory*, vol. 8, no. 1, 1969, pp. 3–53.

Bhattacharya, Amitra Sudan, *Bankimchandra Jibani* (Bankimchandra: A Biography) (Ananda Publishers, Calcutta, 1991).

Bhattacharya, R.K. and J. Sarkar (eds), *Passage Through Indian Civilization* (Anthropological Survey of India, Calcutta, 2002).

Bhattacharya, Sabyasachi, 'Paradigms Lost: Notes on Social History in India', *Economic and Political Weekly*, vol. XXVIII, nos 14–19, 1982, pp. 692–8.

———— (ed.), *The Mahatma and the Poet: Letters and debates between Gandhi and Tagore, 1915–1941* (NBT, Delhi, 2005, 3rd reprint).

———— (ed.), *Development of Modern Indian Thought and the Social Sciences* (Oxford University Press, New Delhi, 2007).

Bhattacharya, Sabyasachi, Joseph Bara, and Chinna Rao Yagati (eds), *Educating the Nation: Documents on the Discourse of National Education in India 1880–1920* (Kanishka, Jawaharlal Nehru University, Delhi, 2003).

Bose, N.K., *Cultural Anthropology* (Arya Sahitya Bhavan, Calcutta, 1929; reprints 1953, 1963).

————, 'Contact of Cultures', *Calcutta Review*, vol. 54, nos 1–3, 1935.

————, 'Hindu Social Organization', *Visva-Bharati Quarterly*, new series, vol. I, no. 4, 1936.

————, *Fifty Years of Science in India: Progress of Anthropology and Archaeology* (Indian Science Congress, Calcutta, 1963).

———— (ed.), *Peasant Life in India: A Study of Indian Unity and Diversity* (Anthropological Survey of India, Calcutta, 1961).

Breckenridge, Carol and Peter van der Veer (eds), *Orientalism and the Post Colonial Predicament* (University of Pennsylvania, Philadelphia, 1993).

Buckle, H.T., *History of Civilization in England*, 2 vols (J.W. Parker & Son, London, 1857–61).

Chakrabarty, Dipesh, *Provincializing Europe: Post-Colonial Thought and Historical Difference* (Oxford University Press, New Delhi, 2001).

Chattopadhyay, Bankimchandra, *Bankim Rachanavali* (ed.) J.C. Bagal (Sahitya Samsad, Calcutta, 1954).

Chattopadhyay, Gautam, *Awakening in Bengal in Early 19th Century: Selected Documents* (Progressive Publishers, Calcutta, 1965).

Cohn, B.S., *Colonialism and its Forms of Knowledge: The British in India* (Princeton University Press, 1996).

Coomaraswamy, Ananda Kentish, *Arts and Crafts of India and Ceylon* (T.N. Foulis, London, 1913).

————, *Dance of Siva: Fourteen Indian Essays* (Asia Publishing House, Bombay, 1952; first edn 1918).

Coomaraswamy, Ananda Kentish, *What is a Civilization and Other Essays* (Oxford University Press, New York, 1989).

Derrett, Duncan M., *Religions, Law and Institutions in India* (Faber, London, 1968).

Deshpande, Prachi, *Creative Pasts: Historical Memory & Identity in Western India, 1700–1788* (Permanent Black, Delhi, 2007).

'Dinkar', Ram Dhari Singh, *Sanskriti ke Char Adhyay* (1955).

Dirks, Nicholas B., *The Hollow Crown: Ethno-history of an Indian Kingdom* (Cambridge University, New York, 1987).

Dodson, Michael S., *Orientalism, Empire and National Culture: India 1770–1880* (Cambridge University Press, Delhi, 2010).

Elphinstone, Mounstuart, *The History of India* (London, 1841; reprint Allahabad, 1966).

Gandhi, M.K., *The Collected Works of Mahatma Gandhi*, 98 vols (Publications Division, New Delhi, 1999).

Gellner, Ernest, *Nations and Nationalism* (Blackwell, Oxford, 1983).

Gopal, Sarvepalli, *Jawaharlal Nehru: A Biography* (Oxford University Press, New Delhi, 1989).

Grover, V., *Political Thinkers of Modern India* (Deep and Deep Publications, Delhi, 1992), vol. 14.

Heesterman, Jan C., *The Inner Conflict of Tradition* (Chicago University Press, Chicago, 1985).

Hobsbawm, Eric, *Nations and Nationalism since 1780* (Cambridge University Press, Cambridge, 1990).

Huntington, Samuel P., *The Clash of Civilizations and the Remaking of World Order* (Simon and Schuster, New York, 1996).

———, 'The Clash of Civilizations', *Foreign Affairs*, no. 72, 1992–3.

———, 'If Not Civilizations, What?', no. 73, November–December, 1993.

Irschick, Eugene F., *Dialogue and History: Constructing South India, 1795–1895* (Berkeley, University of California Press, 1994).

Kane, P.V., *History of the Dharmasastras* (BORS, Poona, vols II and III, 1973, 1974)

Kejariwal, O.P., *The Asiatic Society of Bengal and the Discovery of India's Past: 1784–1838* (Oxford University Press, New Delhi, 1988).

Khilani, Sunil, *The Idea of India* (Hamish Hamilton, London, 1997).

Krishna, Daya, *Prologomena to Any Future Historiography of Cultures and Civilizations* (Project of History of Indian Science, Philosophy and Culture and Munshiram Manoharlal, Delhi, 2005).

Kopf, D., *British Orientalism and the Indian Renaissance* (Berkeley, 1969).

Kosambi, D.D., *Introduction to the Study of Indian History* (Popular Prakashan, Bombay, 1956).

————, *Exasperating Essays: Exercises in Dialectical Method* (Popular Book House, Poona, 1957; India Book Exchange, Calcutta, 1977).

————, *The Culture and Civilization of Ancient India in Historical Outline* (Vikas Publishing House, Delhi, 1970; first edn Routledge, London, 1965).

————, *Myth and Reality* (Popular Prakashan, Bombay, 1962).

Krishna, Daya, *Prologomena to Any Future Historiography of Cultures and Civilizations* (Project of History of Indian Science Philosophy and Culture, M.Manoharlal, Delhi, 2005).

Kroeber, A.L., *An Anthropologist Looks at History* (University of California Press, Berkeley, 1963).

————, *Styles and Civilizations* (Greenwood Press, West Port, CT, 1973).

Kulkarni, A.R. (ed.), *History in Practice: Historians and Sources of Mediaeval Deccan and Marathas* (Books & Books, Delhi, 1993).

Lyall, Alfred C., *The Rise and Expansion of British Dominion in India* (London, 1911; 5th edn).

Maitreya, Akshay Kumar, *Sirajuddaulah* (De's Publishers, Calcutta, 2006, first edn 1897).

————, 'The Black Hole Story', *Journal of the Calcutta Historical Society*, vol. XII, part I, no. 23, pp. 156–71.

Majeed, J., 'James Mill's "The History of British India" and Utilitarianism as a Rhetoric of Reform', *Modern Asian Studies*, vol. 24, no. 2, 1990, pp. 209–24.

————, *Ungoverned Imaginings: James Mill's The History of British India and Orientalism* (Clarendon Press, Oxford, 1992).

Marriott, Mackim, 'Little Communities in an Indigenous Civilization', in MacKim Marriott (ed.), *Village India* (University of Chicago Press, 1955).

Marriott, Mackim, and Bernard S. Cohn, 'Networks and Centres in Integration of Indian civilization', *Journal of Social Research*, Ranchi, vol. I, no. 1, 1958, pp. 1–9.

Michaels, Axel (ed.), *The Pandit* (New Delhi, Manohar, 2001)

Mill, James, *The History of British India* (Baldwin, Cradock, and Joy, London, 1817).

Moir, M.I., D.M. Peers, and Lynn Zastoupil (eds), *J.S. Mill's Encounter with India* (University of Toronto Press, Toronto).

Mookerji, Radha Kumud, *The Fundamental Unity of India* (Bharatiya Vidya Bhavan and Chronicle Books, 2003; first published in London, 1914).

Mujeeb, M., *Indian Muslims* (London, 1962).

Mukerjee, Hiren, *Vivekananda and Indian Freedom* (Calcutta, 1986).

Nagel, Thomas, *The View from Nowhere* (Clarendon Press, Oxford, 1986).

Nandy, Ashis, 'History's Forgotten Doubles', *History and Theory*, vol. 34, no. 2, May 1995, pp. 44–66.

Nehru, Jawaharlal, *The Discovery of India* (Signet Press, Calcutta, 1946; John Day, New York, 1946).

———, *Selected Works of Jawaharlal Nehru* (Nehru Memorial Fund).

O'Hanlon, Rosalind and David Washbrook, 'After Orientalism: Culture, Criticism and Politics in the Third World', *Comparative Studies in Society and History*, vol. 34, no. 1, 1992, pp. 141–84.

Panikkar, K.M., *A Survey of Indian History* (Asia Publication, Bombay, 1954; 1st edn, 1947).

———, *Geographical Factors in Indian History* (Bharatiya Vidya Bhawan, Bombay, 1959).

Paranjape, V.G., and N.B. Utgikar (eds), *Collected Works of Sir R.G. Bhandarkar*, 4 vols (Bhandarkar Oriental Research Institute, Puna, 1928–33).

Pollock, Sheldon, 'Deep Orientalism?', in Carol Breckenridge and Peter Van der Veer (eds), *Orientalism and the Post Colonial Predicament* (Philadelphia, University of Pennsylvania, 1993).

Prakash, Gyan, 'Writing Post-Orientalist Histories of the Third World', *Comparative Studies in Society and History*, vol. 32, no. 2, 1990, pp. 383–408.

———, '*Orientalism* Now', *History and Theory*, vol. 34, no. 3, 1995, pp. 199–212.

Ranade, M.G., *Miscellaneous Writings of the Late Mr Justice M.G Ranade* (Manoranjan Press, Bombay, 1915).

———, *Rise of the Maratha Power* (ed.) R.P. Parvardhan and R.V.Otutkar (Bombay University, Bomaby, 1959).

———, *Rise of the Maratha Power* (Bombay University, 1959).

Rao, Velcheru Narayana, David Shulman, and Sanjay Subrahmanyam, *Textures of Time: Writing History in South India, 1600–1800* (Permanent Black, Delhi, 2001).

Ray, Rajat Kanta, *The Felt Community: Commonality and Mentality before the Emergence of Indian Nationalism* (Oxford University Press, New Delhi, 2003).

Redfield, Robert, 'The Folk Society', *American Journal of Sociology*, vol. 52, no. 4, January 1947, pp. 293–308.

————, *Human Nature and the Study of Society: The Papers Robert Redfield* (ed.) Margaret Park Redfield (Chicago, Chicago University Press, 1962).

Rendall, Jane, 'Scottish Orientalism: From Robertson to James Mill', *The Historical Journal*, vol. 25, no. 1, 1982, pp. 43–63.

Robinson, Andrew and Krishna Dutta (eds), *Rabindranath Tagore, The Myriad-minded Man* (Bloomsbury, London, 1996).

Saha, Gorachand (ed.), *Rabindra Patrabali* (Visva-Bharati, Calcutta, 1984).

Savarkar, V.D., *Hindu-pad-padshahi or a Review of the Hindu Empire of Marathas* (Pune, 1925).

Sen, Amartya, *On Interpreting India's Past* (Asiatic Society, Calcutta, 1996).

————, *The Idea of Justice* (Allen Lane, London, 2009).

Sen, Surendra Nath, *Eighteen Fifty-seven* (New Delhi, 1957).

Singer, Milton (ed.), *Traditional India: Structure and Change* (American Folklore Society, Philadelphia, 1959).

Sinha, Surajit C., 'Tribal Cultures of Peninsular India as a Dimension of the Little Tradition', in Singer (ed.), *Traditional India*.

Skinner, Quentin, 'Meaning and Understanding in the History of Ideas', *History and Theory*, vol. 8, no. 1, 1969, pp. 3–53.

Smith, Anthony D., *The Antiquity of Nations* (Polity, Cambridge, UK, 2004).

Smith, Vincent, *Oxford History of India* (Oxford university Press, Oxford, 1919).

Spengler, Oswald, *The Decline of the West*, English translation (Knopf, New York, 1926; reprint, Oxford University Press, New York, 1991).

Sri Aurobindo, *The Renaissance in India and Other Essays on Indian Culture* (Aurobindo Ashram, Pondicherry, 1947).

————, *The Foundations of Indian Culture* (New York, 1953).

Srinivas, M.N., *Religion and Society among the Coorgs of India* (Clarendon Press, Oxford, 1952).

Swami Vivekananda, *Complete Works of Swami Vivekananda*, 9 vols (Advaita Ashrama, Calcutta, 2008).

Tagore, Rabindranath, *Crisis in Civilization* (Calcutta: Visva-Bharati, 1941; reprint 1964)

————, *Itihas* (Visva-Bharati, Calcutta, 1955).

————, *Nationalism* (ed.) E.P.Thompson (Papermac, London, 1992).

————, *The English Writings of Rabindranath Tagore* (ed.) Sisir Kumar Das (Sahitya Academi, Delhi, 1996; first published by Macmillan, New York, 1917)

————, *Rabindra Rachanabali*, 31 vols (Visva-Bharati, Santiniketan, years).

Thapar, Romila, *Interpreting Early India* (Oxford University Press, New Delhi, 1992).

———, *Time as a Metaphor of History: Early India* (Oxford University Press, New Delhi, 1996).

Toynbee, Arnold J., *A Study of History*, 12 vols. (Oxford University Press, Oxford, 1934-1961).

Tzoref-Ashkenzai, Chen, 'India and the Identity of Europe: The Case of Frederick Schlegel', *Journal of the History of Ideas*, vol. 67, no. 4, 2006, pp. 713–34.

Warder, Anthony K., *Introduction to Indian Historiography* (Popular Prakashan, Bombay, 1972).

———, *Indian Kavya Literature*, 7 vols (Motilal Banarasidass, Delhi, 1971–2004).

Wagoner, P.B., 'Pre-colonial Intellectuals and the Production of Colonial Knowledge', *Comparative Studies in Society and History*, vol. 45, no. 4, 2003, pp. 783–814.

Williams, Raymond, *Culture and Society, 1780–1950* (Chatto & Windus, London, 1958; reprint 1982).

Wittgenstein, Ludwig, *Philosophical Investigations* (trans. G.E.M. Anscombe, New York, Macmillan, 1973).

Wooddroffe, J., *Is India Civilized?* (Ganesh and Co., Madras, 1918).

Index

hegemony 60
identity 74
movement in Bengal 97
and spiritual degradation of Indians 60
stagnation 91
unity 74, 128, 131

dar-ul-Islam 140
Dawn Society's Magazine 125
Daya Krishna 120–2
Deccan College 40
Deccan Education Society 93
Deccan Sabha 38
Deccan Vernacular Translation Society
    6, 93–4
Derozio, Henry Louis Vivian 26
Derrett, Duncan 27
Desai, Mahadev 61
Deshmukh, C.D. 127
Deshpande, Madhav M. 27
development, civilizational trajectories 10
dharma 77–8, 140
    and *dharma-tantra*, conflict 76
Dharmashastras 9, 27, 130
Dinkar, Ramdhari Sinha 90
Dirks, Nicholas 158–9
diversity, religious, ethnic and cultural 6,
    74, 89, 101, 122–3, 137
Dodson, Michael 153
Dravidian culture 123
Duff, Grant 95
    History of the Mahrattas 95
Dutt, Michael Madhusudan 28
Dutt, R.C. 56

East India Company 3, 6, 16, 19–20, 22,
    23, 26, 27
economic principles and laws 55
Elphinstone, Mountstuart 20, 25, 26
    History of British Power in the East 21
    History of India 21
Engels, Frederick, 55
'English knowledge' 3
environmental conditions 29
environmentalists' concern 55
essentialism 51, 59
European(s) 17, 103

cultivation of science 33
Enlightenment 68, 76, 79
supremacy, 32–4

factory system of production, 62–3
family resemblance, notion of 121
Farquahar, J.N. 105
fascism 79
foreign conquest and subjugation 15
France
    British victory over 18
    Revolution (1789) 76, 79

Gandhi, M.K. 1, 2, 3, 4, 5, 9, 38, 40, 47,
    75, 78, 82, 88, 91, 111, 112, 113,
    118, 132, 136, 150
    nationalist discourse of civilization
    47–64
    and Tagore, debate 62, 75
Gandhi Seva Sangh 62
Geddes, Patrick 136
Gellner, Ernest 10, 144
Germany, unification 34
Ghose, Aurobindo 7, 8, 107–11
Ghurye, G.S. 10, 137, 141
    Cities and Civilization 136
    Culture and Society 136
    Occidental Civilization 136
Gibbon, Edward 91
global politics 149
Gobind Singh, Guru 68
Goethe 3, 15
Gokhale, G.K. 38, 42, 53, 61
Goldstucker, Theodor 32
Grihya Sutras 130
Grouset, Rene
    The Civilization of India 87
Gujars 38
Gulf War, First 148–9
Gyan Prakash 152

Harijan 50, 62
Hastings, Warren 24–5, 97
Heesterman, Jan 27
heredity, law of 73
Hill, S.C. 98
Hind Swaraj 1, 3, 4, 47–53, 55, 56